USEFUL TO GOD

Eight lessons from the life of D.L. Moody

JAMES SPENCER

Kingdom Winds

PUBLISHING

USEFUL TO GOD: Eight lessons from the life of D.L. Moody

©Copyright 2022, James Spencer - jamesgspencer.com

All rights reserved. No part of this publication may be reproduced, distributed, or transmitted in any form or by any means, including photocopying, recording, or other electronic or mechanical methods, without the prior written permission of the publisher, except in the case of brief quotations embodied in critical reviews and certain other noncommercial uses permitted by copyright law. For permission requests, write to the publisher at publishing@kingdomwinds.com.

Edited by Karen Dix

Cover Design & Artwork by Justin Stewart - Justifii.com

All Scripture, unless otherwise indicated, is the translation of the author, Dr. James Spencer, from the original Greek and Hebrew texts.

The ESV® Bible (The Holy Bible, English Standard Version®). ESV® Text Edition: 2016. Copyright © 2001 by Crossway, a publishing ministry of Good News Publishers. The ESV® text has been reproduced in cooperation with and by permission of Good News Publishers. Unauthorized reproduction of this publication is prohibited. All rights reserved.

THE HOLY BIBLE, NEW INTERNATIONAL VERSION®, NIV® Copyright © 1973, 1978, 1984, 2011 by Biblica, Inc.® Used by permission. All rights reserved worldwide.

The American Standard Version of the Bible is part of the public domain.

The Holy Bible: International Standard Version. Release 2.0, Build 2015.02.09. Copyright © 1995-2014 by ISV Foundation. ALL RIGHTS RESERVED INTERNATIONALLY. Used by permission of Davidson Press, LLC.

The Holy Bible: International Standard Version. Release 2.0, Build 2015.02.09. Copyright © 1995-2014 by ISV Foundation. ALL RIGHTS RESERVED INTERNATIONALLY. Used by permission of Davidson Press, LLC.

The Holy Bible: International Standard Version. Release 2.0, Build 2015.02.09. Copyright © 1995-2014 by ISV Foundation. ALL RIGHTS RESERVED INTERNATIONALLY. Used by permission of Davidson Press, LLC.

New American Standard Bible®, Copyright © 1960, 1971, 1977, 1995, 2020 by The Lockman Foundation. All rights reserved.

NET Bible® copyright ©1996-2017 All rights reserved. Build 30170414 by Biblical Studies Press, L.L.C.

Premium Color Edition, 2022

ISBN: 978-1-64590-034-4

Published by Kingdom Winds Publishing.

www.kingdomwinds.com

publishing@kingdomwinds.com

Printed in the United States of America.

CONTENTS

01 — PG 4
MEET DWIGHT L. MOODY

02 — PG 14
SURRENDERED

03 — PG 32
PRAYERFUL

04 — PG 48
STUDIOUS

05 — PG 62
HUMBLE

06   PG 78
FREE FROM LOVE OF MONEY

07   PG 94
CONSUMED WITH A PASSION FOR THE LOST

08   PG 112
IMBUED WITH POWER FROM ON HIGH

09   PG 128
UNDISTRACTED

10   PG 150
BECOMING USEFUL TO GOD

INTRODUCTION

At the end of 2018, I was seriously considering leaving Christian work. I was struggling through a challenging year as an academic dean and had nearly lost my sense of God's presence in my life. I was exhausted, angry, and on the verge of hopelessness. After years of pushing myself to achieve, get promotions, and develop a solid reputation within biblical education, I was running on empty (and had been for some time). It was time for a change.

I took a leap of faith away from higher education and accepted a position with Moody Center, a fairly young, independent, Christian non-profit organization that owned a portion of the historic property where Dwight L. Moody lived and did much of his ministry in Northfield, Massachusetts. Stepping into my work there, I was still reeling from a challenging year, but I knew I needed to hit the ground running. In addition to learning the ropes, I also needed to learn about Dwight Moody. Little did I know that the combination of the two would give me something I hadn't had in years: a deep sense of God's presence.

I'd spent my professional career at one of the schools that Moody founded in Chicago, Illinois, so I knew Dwight Moody as an evangelist who had also started Bible institutes. Beyond that, I knew precious little about him. I'd never read any of his books and had only casually thumbed through a few of his biographies. He seemed impressive enough but had never captured my interest.

My relative ignorance about Moody ended up being quite beneficial because I got to know him through reading his personal correspondence that was housed in Moody Center's digital archive project. As I read, Moody began to win me over. His letters were raw with multiple spelling and grammar errors, but they were authentic and written with a clear care and concern for others. Moody was not known as a theological thinker, but in his letters, I discovered a man whose understanding of God influenced the way he interacted with others, shaped his desires and prayers, and handled everyday situations. His letters were not compelling because of his eloquence or his rhetorical prowess but because of his unique ability to convey his faith through more mundane, day-to-day communication. Also, throughout his letters, a certain word that he used to address his desire to be of service to God repeatedly jumped out at me—"useful." With all his heart, Moody strove to be *Useful to God*.

I studied his written works like *Secret Power, Prevailing Prayer: What Hinders It,* and *Pleasure and Profit in Bible Study*. I began to curate a set of Moody quotes and to write some short articles inspired by his life and thought. As I studied Moody's life, I realized I had been too independent, too willing to tie God to my own agendas, and too focused on achievement. Despite earning multiple advanced theological degrees, working in Christian higher education, and being active in my local church, I had lost sight of what it meant to walk by faith.

Now when I reflect on my last few years at Moody Center and the work of God in my life, in part, through my study of Moody, I don't believe God is done with him. God continues to use Moody's story.

This book revisits Moody's life and ministry with the help of one of Moody's contemporaries, R. A. Torrey. Torrey's book, entitled *Why God Used D. L. Moody*, described the characteristics that made Moody radically open to God's use. These characteristics provide a wonderful way to introduce you to Dwight Moody and encourage us to be people who are useful to God.

This book can be enjoyed individually or within a small group setting. After an introduction to Moody, each of the proceeding seven chapters is a journey into the ministry of Moody and how his personal characteristics, the Word, and his work informed his choices. Each chapter also includes a biblical devotion, some probing reflection questions, and the opportunity for you to create your own action plan to grow in the characteristic discussed in the chapter. My hope is that. in considering why God used D. L. Moody, you will be inspired, as I am, to show the world what God can do through an individual who is totally surrendered to him and how we can become such individuals as well.

James Spencer, PhD

01

MEET DWIGHT L. MOODY

What do you know of Dwight L. Moody (1837-1899)? Most people, if they know him at all, know him as an evangelist. He is so much more. Moody is regarded as one of the most significant Christian figures in American history. His influence on Northfield, New England, the United States, and the world is difficult to overestimate.

In his sixty-two short years, Moody was tireless in his service to others in this fallen world. He ministered to soldiers during the Civil and Spanish-American Wars, cared for those made homeless during the Chicago fire, and even tended to cholera patients during an epidemic. He served in various capacities with the YMCA and was influential in the Sunday School movement. He visited numerous cities in the United States, Canada, the United Kingdom, and various other countries to proclaim the gospel.

They called him "Crazy Moody" for holding Sunday school in the slums of Chicago, but nothing kept him from his work as an educator, evangelist, and catalyst of missionary movements. He tried to care for everyone he met and left an enduring mark on the church. Dwight Moody's life and work heavily influenced the Student Volunteer Movement started in 1886, evangelist Billy Graham, and Jesse Overholtzer, the founder of Child Evangelism Fellowship.

Moody spread the gospel of Christ to more than 100 million people and founded five schools, including Northfield Seminary for girls, the Mount Hermon School for boys, the Northfield Bible Training School, the Chicago Bible Institute, and Glasgow Bible College. He held summer conferences that ignited pastors and other Christian workers through worship, prayer, and the preaching of God's word. He was even influential in early Christian publishing efforts as he sought to provide affordable Christian resources to the poor.

Despite being widely respected, not all of Moody's endeavors were well-received. After the Civil War, he was criticized for holding segregated meetings. The African American community, including prominent individuals like Frederick Douglass and Mary McLeod Bethune, expressed more than disappointment in Moody's decision to segregate his meetings in the South. While it seems clear from some of his early interactions with whites in the South that Moody viewed segregation as sinful and rebellious, Moody chose to hold segregated meetings. It is not altogether clear why he made this decision.

Like all of us, Moody had to navigate the changing times. In hindsight, we can easily criticize and question his responses and even demonize and diminish his work because of them. But in truth, Moody was like the rest of us—faithful and flawed. We should not venerate him as a saint, dismiss him as a demon, or deny his faithful contribution to the Kingdom of God. Moody was not used by God because he always made the right decision. Instead, he was used by God despite his shortcomings.

That God used D. L. Moody despite his shortcomings and mistakes reminds us that Moody was never the hero of his story. God is the hero.

In considering the characteristics of D. L. Moody, we must learn to look beyond the man to see God at work. After all, "neither he who plants nor he who waters is anything, but only God who gives the growth" (1 Cor. 3:7 ESV). As we look back on the life and ministry of D. L. Moody, we are not concerned with his marketing strategies or his ability to fundraise. Moody did great things, but those "great" things don't include starting schools, drawing crowds, or funding ministries. The great things Dwight Moody did were also simple things like prayer, study, giving thanks, remaining humble, remaining free from the love of money, and constantly seeking to submit himself to God's will. Such are the great things of faith.

WHY GOD USED D. L. MOODY

In 1923, Moody's friend R. A. Torrey wrote a lengthy pamphlet entitled "Why God Used D. L. Moody." Torrey was a contemporary of Dwight Moody and served alongside him during the Chicago World's Fair. He also helped Moody pastor the Moody Church and served as a superintendent and president of the Chicago Bible Institute. He became the first academic dean of what is now Biola University. Torrey would carry on Moody's evangelistic ministry and became one of the most important evangelists of the early twentieth century.[1]

In his writing, Torrey discusses seven characteristics of Dwight Moody. He suggests that the reason God used D. L. Moody had less to do with Moody's intellect or skill as a speaker and more to do with who Mr. Moody was. It was less about talent than it was about character.

---

1 Fred Sanders, *How God Used R. A. Torrey: A Short Biography as Told Through His Sermons* (Chicago: Moody, 2015).

For Torrey, God used D. L. Moody because Moody was...

SURRENDERED

PRAYERFUL

STUDIOUS

HUMBLE

FREE FROM LOVE OF MONEY

CONSUMED WITH PASSION FOR THE LOST

ENDUED WITH POWER FROM ON HIGH

To Torrey's list, we will add one more characteristic: Moody was a man **UNDISTRACTED FROM THE WORK OF THE KINGDOM**.

Studying these characteristics is not an academic exercise. Instead, in learning about the characteristics that made D. L. Moody uniquely useful to God, the goal is to begin cultivating these characteristics within our own lives. As R. A. Torrey notes, "the God who used D. L. Moody in his day is just as ready to use you and me, in this day, if we, on our part, do what D. L. Moody did, which was what made it possible for God to so abundantly use him."[2] God is not yet done using the man from Northfield, just as he is not done using us. We only need to become the sort of people who are prepared to walk by faith, not by sight (2 Cor. 5:7).

It's important to understand, however, that acquiring Moody's characteristics does not guarantee that we will achieve the sort of success D. L. Moody had during his ministry, nor should that be our goal. God will not necessarily use us to reach multiple millions. Those who look at our lives and ministries might not describe them as "successful." In the eyes of the world, "success" is seldom measured in

---

2 Torrey, *Why God Used D. L. Moody*, 6.

the depth of one's character or the degree to which one has followed the Holy Spirit. Yet for those with eyes to see and ears to hear, we know that the successes of the world are fleeting while the faith of God's people will "result in praise and glory and honor at the revelation of Jesus Christ" (1 Peter 1:7 ESV).

Now to many of us, participating in the body may feel mundane. Being faithful in the moments that seem to have little importance can challenge us. It is easy to look at Moody's ministry or the ministries of those who have national and international platforms today and wonder whether our minimal efforts really matter. Moody offers consolation, saying,

> You say you have not got much; well, you can use what you have. The longer I work in Christ's vineyard, the more convinced I am that a good many are kept out of the service of Christ, deprived of the luxury of working for God because they are trying to do some great thing. Let us be willing to do little things. And let us remember that nothing is small in which God is.[3]

In other words, we are not seeking to become the "next big thing" but to make much of God by allowing him to work in and through us.

Also, we must not only understand Moody's characteristics but also actively put them into practice. Otherwise, they will do little to help you become useful to God. Moody was a man of action. What he knew and understood, he did. While there is nothing wrong with pursuing deep academic study, not all of us have the opportunity or inclination to do so. All of us who follow Christ are disciples and therefore committed to living more like Christ every day. Disciples do not simply store up knowledge; they put that knowledge into practice. As we do this, we trust that we will come to a fuller understanding of the great faithfulness and love of our God.

---

[3] D. L. Moody, *"To the Work! To the Work!" Exhortations to Christians* (Toronto: Rose, 1885), 74.

Finally, remember that cultivating the characteristics of Moody will not make us somehow superior to others within the community of faith or in the world at large. We are not tapping into some secret knowledge or becoming spiritual giants, ascending to heights that mere mortals can never reach. It is quite the opposite. We are not seeking to become the modern-day pharisee who thanks God that he is "not like other men" (Luke 18:11 ESV). Instead, our desire should be to become people who humble ourselves, recalling that, whatever our part in developing these characteristics may be, we have been saved by grace through faith and have no room to boast (Eph. 2:8–9).

If we orient our lives around prayer and Bible study, cultivate humility and a deep concern for the lost, or lean upon the power of the Holy Spirit, we acknowledge the futility of depending on our own finite resources. We commit to passing all glory to God, keeping none for ourselves. As we give all glory to God, we clearly show that our strange, peaceful way of being in the world is made possible by Christ's life, death, and resurrection and by the gift of the Holy Spirit through whom "God may use us mightily in the building up of His Church and hastening His glory."[4]

MOODY'S WORK IN OUR WORLD

Today we live in a world that is not as it is supposed to be. We see war, sickness, poverty, political unrest, slavery, and prejudice, both at home and abroad. Our world is chaotic. It is broken. And we are broken as well. Our desires are misdirected, and we too often live in the world as if God does not exist. As we make our own way, pursue our own goals, and attend to our own concerns, we often imagine that the course of

---

4 D. L. Moody, *Secret Power* (Chicago: F. H. Revell, 1881), 46.

our lives can be determined by our sheer force of will. Yet, to paraphrase Robert Burns, the best laid plans of mice and men do often go astray.[5]

But Moody taught the good news that God has overcome sin and death through the crucifixion of Jesus Christ and that our world will not suffer under sin forever. God will create a new heaven and earth (Isa. 65:17; 2 Pet. 3:13). While we wait for the consummation of God's victory, we must navigate a world in which our own insecurities, fears, and desire for control result in more than everyday tension. They result in war, greed, partiality, and a host of other problems.

God's people are not immune to the difficulties of a fallen world. The church experiences sickness, feels the pain of war, struggles to honor God in times of want and in times of plenty, and wrestles to be impartial. Yet, we do not simply seek to survive this world until Christ returns to make all things new. Like D. L. Moody, we are to proclaim God to the world in word and deed because, as Christians, we are not responsible for fixing the world. We are responsible for living faithfully in a world so broken only God can fix it. As we fulfill that responsibility, we trust God to work through us rather than for us, even though we may not always understand just what God is doing.

Moody knew that as Christians, we are called to live as Christians. We are saved by grace through faith in Christ Jesus (Eph. 2:8–9). We have been declared innocent through Christ's sacrificial death and raised with him to "walk in newness of life" (Rom. 6:4 ESV). That "newness of life" involves freedom from sin not only in the sense that we become capable of living according to the Spirit rather than the flesh but also in the sense that we recognize sin as sin. It is, after all, through the confession of sin that we mark ourselves off as a community committed to truth rather than to perfection (1 John 1:9). We are called to move

---

5 The original quote reads "The best laid schemes o' Mice an' Men, Gang aft agley," is from Robert Burns' poem entitled "To a Mouse." See Robert Burns, *The Collected Works of Robert Burns* (Hertfordshire: Wodsworth, 1994), 110.

from darkness to light, not by becoming morally superior but "by embracing truth (however difficult or inconvenient) and not simply through affirmation and obedience, but through confession, repentance, forgiveness, and reconciliation."[6] By embracing truth, especially when it is inconvenient, Christians open themselves up to being more and more useful to God.

As we seek to proclaim the gospel to a world that needs to hear it, our failures may bring disappointment and discouragement, but our successes can cultivate pride. It's easy to get caught up in our own schemes and push God to the margins of our lives so that the Holy Spirit no longer directs us. He can become little more than a resource we seek to tap to accomplish our own plans. We may try to press God into service to our agendas rather than living as a community of women and men who serve him.

Perhaps our biggest challenge as God's people is to tell a truthful, theological tale by the way we live and work in community instead of succumbing to the world's wisdom, anxieties, politics, or insufficient solutions. Like Moody, we are called to live in a manner that demonstrates our utter belief in God's presence. Even as we navigate a world that does not rightly acknowledge the God of the Old and New Testaments, we show the world what it means to live according to the will and wisdom of God. We must live in it as women and men called from darkness to light. As Moody once said, "In the place God has put us, He expects us to shine, to be living witnesses, to be a bright and shining light. While we are here our work is to shine for Him…"[7]

---

[6] James Spencer, *Thinking Christian: Essays on Testimony, Accountability, and the Christian Mind* (Self-published, KSP, 2020), 23.
[7] Dwight L. Moody, *Arrows and Anecdotes* (London, Oxford University, 1876), 134.

OUR WORK AS CHRISTIANS

If we desire to be useful to God in this world, we must learn to follow Him with a devotion that showcases both our unreserved dedication to God and our tenacious love for our neighbors (Deut. 6:4-5; Luke 10:27). We must be a community whose uncompromising love for God forms us into a people that "constantly gestures toward joining, toward the desire to hear, to know, and to embrace" so as to "mirror God's own seeking of the creation and of the creature turned away from the divine voice."[8]

To be useful to God in this world, we must surely look to the Scriptures as the final authority for life and faith. But we must also look to those who have come before us. In Hebrews 11, we find that we have a faithful legacy upon which we can look back. The faith demonstrated in the lives of those who walked with God before us encourages us to

> …lay aside every weight, and sin which clings so closely, and let us run with endurance the race that is set before us, looking to Jesus, the founder and perfecter of our faith, who for the joy that was set before him endured the cross, despising the shame, and is seated at the right hand of the throne of God (Heb. 12:1–2 ESV).

As we consider those holy people who contribute to that "cloud of witnesses" today, we surely remember Abraham, Isaac, Jacob, Joseph, Moses, Rahab, and many other women and men whose acts of faith are recorded in the Bible (Heb. 12:1). Yet, we would also do well to remember those, like Dwight L. Moody, who is not mentioned in the scripture but whose life and ministry remind us that God continues to demonstrate His power and glory through the lives of those prepared to be used by Him.

---
8 Willie James Jennings, *The Christian Imagination: Theology and the Origins of Race* (New Haven: Yale University Press, 2010), 291.

02

SURRENDERED

> "A great many people are afraid of the will of God, and yet I believe that one of the sweetest lessons that we can learn in the school of Christ is the surrender of our wills to God, letting Him plan for us and rule our lives."
>
> – D. L. Moody,
> *Men of the Bible*

After my first attempt at entering ministry failed miserably, I found myself unemployed without any prospects. It wasn't a great feeling. I'd spent a fair amount of money and a great deal of time earning two graduate degrees in theological studies and completing my doctoral coursework. I still had a long way to go to finish my dissertation and was beginning to wonder if it was worth the effort.

I hated being vulnerable. Life was out of my control, and there seemed to be precious little that I could do about it. After about a year of being out of work, I got a job in online education at a Bible college in Chicago, IL. Unfortunately, it wasn't exactly stable. In addition to rumors that there were plans to shut down the department or lay off staff, many faculty members, including some of those who had been my professors, viewed online education as substandard. Those feelings of vulnerability began to surface again. I gave myself over to them.

Over the next several years, I delayed finishing my dissertation, adopted a grueling pace at work, and ignored my family. While some might have seen me as ambitious, I wasn't. I was just trying to avoid the vulnerability and uselessness I'd felt when I spent a year without a job. I had decided that the only way to preserve my sense of security was to succeed at all costs. I knew what it would take to be secure. I knew what it would take to become indispensable at work. I adopted the logic of the system and surrendered to it. In giving myself over to the logic of the system, I was seeking security and hoping for meaning. Yet, I was dependent on others for my security. I needed to be useful to them.

I made a mistake. In my efforts to avoid feeling vulnerable, I surrendered to a way of life that had less to do with honoring God or discerning his will and more to do with serving my own needs and wants in my own way. As I've reflected on that time in my life, what I've realized is that we always surrender to something. As Paul notes in Romans 6:16 (ESV), we are either slaves to "sin, which leads to death," or we are slaves to "obedience, which leads to righteousness." By choosing to surrender to a world of constant performance that demanded continual success, I was ignoring God and denying his wisdom. That had to change. I had to begin trusting God by obeying him even when obeying him didn't make any sense. That is the essence of what it means to be surrendered. We obey God even when doing so comes with a cost.

SURRENDER IN SCRIPTURE

Throughout the Old and New Testaments, we see the folly of those who fail to surrender to God's will and instead lean on their own understanding and resources. We see examples of people who act based on their own limitations. Even when those limitations become painfully obvious, they continue to resist the Lord. They refuse to surrender to him and his way of life.

Consider the Pharaoh of the Exodus, "who did not know Joseph" (Exod. 1:8 ESV). Pharaoh was unaware of the blessing that God brought to Egypt through Joseph and would bring through the Israelites who settled in Goshen. Pharaoh saw the Hebrews as a resource and a growing threat. Despite being regarded as a god in Egypt, Pharaoh was nothing more than a human being. He was dependent on labor to produce crops. He was concerned about the stability and security of Egypt. As he looked out upon the Hebrews who continued to "be fruitful and multiply" (Gen. 1:28 ESV; Exod. 1:7), he did not see God's blessing but a threat to the fragile nation he ruled (Exod. 1:10). When God speaks to Pharaoh through Moses, Pharaoh refuses to surrender his position and becomes determined to oppose God rather than submit to God's wisdom and will.

Pharaoh's refusal to accept God's presence was rooted in his ignorance of Joseph. He could not understand how the growth and prosperity of the Hebrews could be a blessing to Egypt. Even when God sent plagues upon Egypt, Pharaoh refused to submit. He refused to consider the possibility that surrendering to the Lord would be infinitely better than ruling Egypt on his own terms. His ignorance and hard-hearted response kept him from realizing that God desired to bless the nations through his people as he had done through Joseph. In opposing God and refusing to surrender, Pharaoh and his nation are brought to ruin.

Israel also needed to learn to surrender. After being brought out of Egypt, Israel was to be a nation ruled not by Pharaoh but by God. God has no need for the unceasing labor of slaves. Even in the wilderness, he is never without resources to care for his people. It was in the wilderness that God taught Israel that "man does not live by bread alone, but man lives by every word that comes from the mouth of the Lord" (Deut. 8:3 ESV). Unfortunately, Israel's history does not always suggest that they learned this lesson well. Too often, Israel's leadership and people sought to make their own way while placating God. They did not learn surrender.

MOODY'S SURRENDER

To be "surrendered" means to commit to reorienting our way of being in the world to demonstrate our allegiance to God. We must commit to living by faith rather than by sight (2 Cor. 5:7). In his discussion of Abraham's four surrenders, D. L. Moody notes, "People are constantly walking by sight, lured by the temptations of men and of the world. Men are very anxious to get their sons into lucrative positions, although it may be disastrous to their character; it may ruin them morally and religiously, and in every other way. The glitter of this world seems to attract them."¹

As we look at the blessings we have received, we should not be prideful but thankful (Deut. 8:17–18). As we see the resources God has given to others, we should not seek to bring them under our own control but to be content with God's provision (Exod. 20:15, 17; Deut. 5:19, 21; Phil. 4:11–13). When we are asked to trade our convictions for riches and success, we must stand firm, knowing that the treasures of this world are fleeting (Matt. 6:19–21). When we face trials, we must do so with a peace that the world cannot understand and a joy that desires God's refining work within us (Phil. 4:7; James 1:2–4). We should seek truth and do justice without partiality (Lev. 19:15). We should not "repay evil for evil or reviling for reviling, but on the contrary, bless, for to this you were called, that you may obtain a blessing" (1 Pet. 3:9 ESV).

Surely our physical eyes are not the real problem. Seeing the world clearly is a matter of perspective. So, we must adopt a new posture within the world that seeks God first and faithfully reflects his glory. Moody's life showed us that being surrendered is not about being inactive but about being willing to accept God's will even when it runs counter to our own. As Moody notes,

> I cannot look into the future. I do not know what is going to happen tomorrow; in fact, I do not know what may happen before night; so I cannot choose for myself as well as God can choose for me, and it is much better to surrender my will to God's will.²

In surrendering, we open ourselves up to a new realm of possibilities rooted in our belief in a wise, sovereign, and benevolent God. We are no longer slaves to frenzied activities aimed at fixing the world but can participate with God through prayer, fasting, lament, worship, and

---

1 D. L. Moody, *Men of the Bible* (Chicago: Bible Institute Colportage Association, 1898), 13.
2 Moody, *Men of the Bible*, 7.

confession. By surrendering ourselves fully to God, we will find our possibilities expanded beyond the logic of our times and our own personal limitations because "Christians charged with nothing but obedience are freed for obedience."[3] We no longer need a plan to fix the world; we only have to live faithfully in a world so broken only God can fix it.

THE BATTLE TO SURRENDER

Surrendering to God is not easy. It certainly wasn't easy for Dwight Moody. Moody sought to be a man fully surrendered to the Lord, yet surrendering to the Lord is, unfortunately, a struggle. As Moody himself admits, "whenever God has been calling me to higher service, there has always been a conflict with my will. I have fought against it, but God's will has been done instead of mine."[4] He goes on to offer examples from those moments throughout his life when he battled God's will, noting,

> When I came to Jesus Christ, I had a terrible battle to surrender my will, and to take God's will. When I gave up business, I had another battle for three months…when God was calling me…to go out and preach the gospel all over the land, instead of staying in Chicago. I fought against it for months…[5]

We should not expect to surrender once and for all. If our experience is anything like Moody's, we can anticipate an ongoing struggle to accept God's will. We are often stubborn, and our desire to chart our own course is frequently too strong. Yet, the struggle to surrender cannot be attributed to our hardheartedness or hardheadedness alone. God has given us the capacity to think, to reason, and to converse. We will often struggle to surrender because we are seeking to understand God and his ways. In such moments, we are not stubborn but unaware of just what God is doing and how he desires us to take part in what he is doing.

---

[3] Jonathan Tran, *The Vietnam War and Theologies of Memory: Time and Eternity in the Far Century* (Malden: Blackwell, 2010), 8.
[4] Moody, *Men of the Bible*, 23.
[5] Moody, *Men of the Bible*, 23-24.

But whether we struggle because we tend to be rebellious or because of our ongoing quest to understand, surrender is a beautiful thing. It is worth the struggle. In surrender, we admit our limitations and the limitations of humanity in general and commit to developing a deep sensitivity to looking at the world with eyes that see and listening to the world with ears that hear. As Dwight Moody professed, "the best thing I ever did was when I surrendered my will and let the will of God be done in me."[6]

THREE STEPS TO SURRENDER

One of the main reasons surrender feels counterintuitive is that we are unaware of God's plan and our role in it. For example, we may be tempted to give in to our evangelical impulses in the moment and insist upon immediate action, decision, and perfection from others. However, it's all too easy to confuse winning supporters with making true change or to adopt hasty judgments on current biblical, theological, or ethical issues over the hard-won and carefully stated insight from the past.[7]

As Moody's life makes clear, surrender does not require inactivity. It requires sensitivity. It requires our willingness to revise our thinking in response to the prompting of the Holy Spirit. In a very real sense, the Christian community has no other agenda than "to do justice, and to love kindness, and to walk humbly with your God" (Mic. 6:8 ESV). When we lose sight of the basic goal of following the Lord, we may end up "forcing the 'right' result without submitting to the transformative work of God."[8]

---

6 Moody, *Men of the Bible*, 24.
7 This section echoes Noll's discussion of "built-in barriers to productive thinking" that continue to plague evangelicalism which "include an immediatism that insists on action, decision, and even perfection right now; a populism that confuses winning supporters with mastering actually existing situations; and an antitraditionalism that privileges current judgments on biblical, theological, and ethical issues (however hastily formed) over insight from the past (however hard-won and carefully stated)" (Mark A. Noll, *Jesus Christ and the Life of the Mind* [Grand Rapids: Eerdmans, 2011], 152).
8 Spencer, *Thinking Christian*, 162.

STEP 1: **PREPARE TO SURRENDER.**

Surrender requires preparation. Like most of our other decisions, the decision to surrender is seldom made at the spur of the moment. The choices we make are often influenced by how well prepared we are to make them at a given moment. As theologian Samuel Wells notes, "The time for moral effort is the time of formation and training…The point of this effort is to form skills and habits—habits that mean people take the right things for granted and skills that give them ability to do the things they take for granted."[9] In other words, while important, the moment of decision is often informed by our preparations beforehand. Like an athlete who puts in hours at the gym preparing for a competition, Christians cannot separate the process of preparation from the moment of decision.

However, preparing to surrender isn't always an option. For example, Abram was not prepared to respond to God's call to "Go from your country, your people and your father's household to the land I will show you" (Gen. 12:1 NIV). Yet if we have dedicated our lives to Christ, we should be somewhat prepared to surrender when the moment comes to do so. We don't prepare as a means to an end. Instead, we prepare because if we don't, we are not truly living as Christians. Having been united with Christ in his death and resurrection, how else could we demonstrate our new identity if not by continually turning away from a "mind governed by the flesh" and toward a "mind governed by the Spirit" (Rom. 8:6 NIV)?

STEP 2: **EMBRACE THE STRUGGLE.**

Adapting to the Christian life is not always easy. Trusting God is not something we do in a vacuum. Instead, we do it in an environment where falsehood runs rampant and the pressures of day-to-day living press in on

---

9 Samuel Wells, *Improvisation: The Drama of Christian Ethics* (Grand Rapids: Baker Academic, 2018), 55.

us. We are consistently tempted to busy ourselves like Martha rather than sitting at the feet of Jesus like Mary (Luke 10:38-42). We aren't asked to surrender in a warm, safe place where we have no cares or worries. We are asked to surrender amid the worries and anxieties of a broken world that tempt us to chase after the urgencies of the moment rather than choosing to "seek first the kingdom of God and his righteousness" (Matt. 6:33 ESV).

As Moody described his experience with surrender as a struggle, so we can also expect to fight against setting aside our own plans and desires to follow God's leading. We will likely wrestle with God as we try to understand where he wants us to go. Even so, the struggle is not a sign of weakness. It is part of a process that draws us ever closer to the Lord.

STEP 3: REIMAGINE LIFE IN SURRENDER.

What possibilities are we missing when we refuse to surrender to God? What would the world look like if we stopped trying to get God to do what we want him to do and let him determine what we should do? Seeing the world with God in control is crucial to our ability to surrender because we know that God is not constrained by the challenges and limitations we face. As the psalmist notes,

> O Lord God of hosts, who is mighty as you are, O Lord, with your faithfulness all around you? You rule the raging of the sea; when its waves rise, you still them. You crushed Rahab like a carcass; you scattered your enemies with your mighty arm. The heavens are yours; the earth also is yours; the world and all that is in it, you have founded them (Ps. 89:8–11 ESV).

God is not constrained by the world's economics, politics, organizations, cultures, or logic. He is active within history but never subject to it. Nothing in this world has the power to impose its will on God and to keep him from achieving his purposes. We can surrender because we serve a God for whom "one day is as a thousand years, and a thousand years as one day" (2 Peter 3:8 ESV). Time is not even an obstacle for God.

We accept that our role is not necessarily to achieve what the world sees as success but to bear the "marks of Jesus" on our bodies as signs of our faithful ministry (Gal. 6:17 ESV). It is through our weakness that God's "power is made perfect" (2 Cor. 12:9 ESV). Ultimately, we recognize that the one who is proclaimed worthy is not the conquering hero of myth and legend but the "Lamb who was slain" (Rev. 5:12 ESV). Even God's victories defy the common logic of the world.

As we look upon the world with "unsurrendered" eyes, we will find ourselves dependent on our own abilities. We tend to develop "ends and means," thinking to justify our own agendas and ambitions. We even make our legitimate concerns into "a screen between God and us."[10] God begins to occupy the margins of our lives rather than standing front and center.

Surrendered eyes see the world differently. They see the importance of waiting on God, following him, and allowing him to redirect and refine our desires. They see the necessity within a fallen world for the urgent activities of worship, prayer, lament, study, and deliberation. They see a world in which we must carve out "a space to have the sort of slow, deliberate dialogues that reflect our deep conviction that discerning the Spirit is crucial to offering faithful testimony."[11]

---

10 Bruce Ellis Benson, *Graven Ideologies: Nietzsche, Derrida and Marion on Modern Idolatry* (Downers Grove: InterVarsity, 2002), 18.
11 Spencer, *Thinking Christian*, 174.

To surrender is to commit to seeing God, the world, and ourselves in new ways. As we surrender, we will find ourselves in the position to see what God will do with the women and men who have given themselves up wholly to him. And the result will be "more than all we ask or imagine" (Eph. 3:20 NIV).

WALK IN THE WORD

"If you obey the commandments of the LORD your God that I command you today, by loving the LORD your God, by walking in his ways, and by keeping his commandments and his statutes and his rules, then you shall live and multiply, and the LORD your God will bless you in the land that you are entering to take possession of it."

– Deuteronomy 30:16 ESV

THE GOD WHOSE WAYS WE DESIRE TO KNOW

There are some in today's church who have a misconception about the Old Testament. They believe that the Old Covenant is a covenant of works and that Israel's obedience was intended to secure God's blessing. They believe that Israel was simply obeying as a covenant obligation that would ultimately result in blessing instead of acting out of an allegiance to God. This misconception has led some in the church to suggest that the Old Testament is unnecessary. Yet if we set aside the Old Testament with all its strangeness and oddities, we will miss opportunities to be strange and odd in the world.

The old covenant, like the new, requires obedience that springs from love and faith. In Deuteronomy 30:11-20, Moses speaks to the people of Israel. On the cusp of entering the Promised Land, Moses reminds them of the commands God has given and how he has brought them close to the people: "But the word is very near you. It is in your mouth and in your heart, so that you can do it" (Deut. 30:14 ESV).

Obedience will bring blessing, but the covenant is not a barter system. God is not asking for obedience in exchange for blessing. One is not payment for the other. Instead, he is pointing out the way of things. Obeying God's commands is about accepting the truth of God's position in the world and living in light of his wisdom. Blessing flows from obedience. While that blessing may not be tangible or immediate, obedience as an outworking of our love for God will enrich our lives in ways we won't suspect and cannot always fathom.

Life comes through obedience not because God will reward us for our ability to follow the rules he has set forth but because in keeping his commands, we show ourselves willing to walk in the ways of life. To "choose life" is to accept the fact that God "is your life and length of days" (Deut. 30:19–20 ESV). We obey God not because we seek his gifts but because we know of no other way to live in the presence of a Holy God whose love "never ceases and mercies never come to an end" (Lam. 3:22).

If we are to walk in the ways of God, we must understand the ways of God. We must study not to fill our heads with knowledge but to reshape our hearts and minds so that we begin to see the world as God sees it and to see him move within it. Through the study of the Old and New Testaments, we have opportunities to reimagine the world in ways that might affect the way we live in it. We study to be transformed, to learn God's ways, and to commit more fully to loving God.

To become a person whose "delight is in the law of the Lord" (Ps. 1:2 ESV), we must commit to learning his word, submit our thoughts to it as the final authority for life and faith, and live in a manner that demonstrates our conviction that all God has said is true. As we study the Old and New Testaments, we will learn the ways of God and be prepared to walk in them. The more we walk in them, the more we will understand the wisdom God has given us.

We must see obedience to God as freeing, not oppressive. By obeying God, we set aside any reliance on the things of this world, knowing that death awaits us if we "turn aside and do not obey but are lured away to worship and serve other gods" (Deut. 30:17). There is one path to follow in this life, and it is a path set forth by a God who desires us to experience life in his presence. In the end, we desire to know God's ways because they lead us to him.

REFLECTION QUESTIONS

01 | How might you respond to someone who thinks we should abandon the Old Testament?

02 | How is obedience related to blessing?

03 | What is the relationship between obedience and life? Why does following other gods bring death?

04 | How might this understanding of obedience align with the reference to the "obedience of faith" in Romans 1:5?

05 | Should we always expect tangible blessings (health and wealth) when we obey?

06 | How might we go about cultivating a desire to know the ways of God? To what extent do you agree with the suggestions regarding study?

07 | Having read about this characteristic of Dwight L. Moody, do you feel you have surrendered your life to God? Why or why not?

08 | If not, which step of the surrender process (pgs. 22 – 23) do you struggle with most and why?

To move towards becoming more "surrendered," I will:

03

PRAYERFUL

"My experience is that those who pray most in their closets generally make short prayers in public. Long prayers are too often not prayers at all, and they weary the people."

— D. L. Moody,
Prevailing Prayer: What Hinders It

Prayer is deeply connected to surrender and submission. As Moody notes, "All true prayer must be offered in full submission to God."[1] For Moody, prayer is done with God's will in mind, and if it is not informed by the Scriptures, "we shall be ignorant of the mind and will of God, and become mystical and fanatical, and liable to be blown about by every wind of doctrine."[2] When we pray, we do not simply seek to have our petitions answered. Rather, in prayer, we admit our utter dependence upon the Lord to restore order to a chaotic world.

When prayer does not seek God's will, it can become empty and misused. Prayer is meant to humble us, yet it can also be used to showcase our piety (Luke 20:47) or to reinforce an inflated self-perception (Luke 18:11). As easy as it may be to glamorize prayer, we would be mistaken to think that any approach to prayer will conform us more closely to the image of Christ. Moody recognizes as much when he quotes an unknown source who notes,

> …prayer does not mean that I am to bring God down to my thoughts and my purposes, and bend His government according to my foolish, silly, and sometimes sinful notions…I am afraid sometimes we think of prayer as altogether of an opposite character, as if thereby we persuaded or influenced our Father in heaven to do whatever comes into our own minds, and whatever would accomplish our foolish, weak-sighted purposes.[3]

BEING PRAYERFUL

To be prayerful involves an openness to God and his will. Our prayers should prompt us to glorify God. Prayer is not a vehicle for us to manipulate God or to impose our will on him but to express our desire

---

1 D. L. Moody, *Prevailing Prayer: What Hinders It?* (Chicago: F. H. Revell, 1884), 102.
2 Moody, *Prevailing Prayer*, 4.
3 Moody, *Prevailing Prayer*, 102-103.

that God's will be done "on earth as it is in heaven" (Matt. 6:10). To be prayerful means, in part, that we bring our petitions to God, knowing and hoping that God, the giver of good gifts (Matt. 7:10–12), will not give us what we think we want but rather what will accomplish his purposes.

Sadly, prayer is not immune to human sinfulness. We do not lose our blind spots or misunderstandings when we pray. We bring our own concerns and agendas with us to our prayers. Our concerns and agendas can motivate us to pray for all the wrong reasons. They can become the way we seek to conform the world to our own image as we impress upon others our own skewed notions about the way the world is supposed to be. Prayer can "become a way of glossing gossip with piety…instead of principally a means of communicating with God."[4] Our prayers can become like those "confident of their own righteousness" who "looked down on everyone else" (Luke 18:9 NIV). If we find ourselves praying like the Pharisee who thanks God that he is "not like other people—robbers, evildoers, adulterers—or even like this tax collector" (Luke 18:11 NIV), we can be sure we are being more prideful than prayerful.

We must take care to ensure that our prayers do not become self-serving. We do not pray in ways that attempt to manipulate or bargain with God. We must always be on our way to expressing our desire to see God's will done in our individual and collective lives. We should not use prayer to improve our position in this life or to degrade others. We should use it to express our desire to have God-determined lives.

As Moody notes, "In former years, I was very ambitious [sic] to get rich; I used to pray for one hundred thousand dollars; that was my aim, and I used to say, 'God does not answer my prayer; He does not make me rich.'"[5] Moody's reflection on his early prayer life illustrates the sort of misdirected desire we often bring to our prayers. It is possible for us to

---

4 Winner, *The Dangers of Christian Practice*, 68.
5 Moody, *Secret Power*, 65-66.

pray in a way that makes it seem as if God serves us. Moody admits that in his prayer for wealth, he "had no warrant for such a prayer; yet a good many people pray in that way; they think that they pray, but they do not pray according to the Scriptures. The Spirit of God has nothing to do with their prayers, and such prayers are not the product of His teaching."[6]

LEARNING TO PRAY

Prayer is not simply a means for achieving our own ends but is an end in itself. When we pray, we certainly expect God to answer our prayers (in whatever unexpected ways He chooses!), but we are also presenting ourselves as people of prayer. To become people of prayer, praying must become less of a chore and more of a natural practice. How else can we rightfully acknowledge God's wisdom, benevolence, and authority? When we pray for God's will to be done, we give ourselves over to God. We trust not only that God freely operates within the world but that He knows best what needs to be done to work "for the good of those who love him, who have been called according to his purpose" (Rom. 8:28 NIV).

Prayer is indispensable for Christians. Through prayer, we face the challenges of living in a fallen world. When we pray with a spirit submitted to God, and when we desire to see Him move in the world even more than we desire our own comforts or ambitions, our prayer helps us to see the world rightly. Our goal should be for prayer to become as natural as breathing.

As the theologian Stanley Hauerwas puts it, "God has given us a wonderful exercise for training in truthfulness. That exercise is called prayer."[7] Prayer reminds us that it is indeed possible to live a life of obedience and faith

---

6 Moody, *Secret Power*, 66.
7 Stanley Hauerwas, *The Character of Virtue: Letters to a Godson* (Grand Rapids: Eerdmans, 2018), 39.

despite the challenges we face in the world. It reminds us that God is with us, available to us, and ready to transform us. Prayer is as simple as a conversation with a God who is always present. Through prayer, Christians "approach God's throne of grace with confidence, so that we may receive mercy and find grace to help us in our time of need" (Heb. 4:16 NIV).

BECOMING A PRAYERFUL PEOPLE

There is a difference between understanding prayer and becoming people of prayer. Prayer is not something we do as an isolated activity. It occurs within the concrete situations of our everyday lives. As such, there are several "elements which are essential to true prayer."[8] These elements remind us that prayer is not some magic incantation but a means of conversing with the God we serve. To call on God in prayer without attending to our broader orientations and actions lacks integrity in so much as we ask God to provide, to forgive, to fix, and to prosper on our terms.

Moody identifies nine elements essential to true prayer. Each element reminds us that prayer is not an isolated practice but exists within a web of other Christian practices that demonstrate our love for God and neighbor. Moody notes adoration, confession, restitution, thanksgiving, forgiveness, unity, faith, petition, and submission among such practices, offering a specific treatment of each. These practices are all expressions of self-sacrifice, humility, and a commitment to mending relationships broken by sin. Moody therefore points to the interrelationship between prayer and the two greatest commandments, which call us to love God with all we have and to love our neighbor as we love ourselves (Matt. 22:34–40).

---

8 Moody, *Prevailing Prayer*, 16.

We must never pray as if God is the fabled genie in a bottle obliged to grant us three wishes. We cannot manipulate God through prayer. Instead, as Moody argues based on Proverbs 28:9 (ESV), the prayer of the one who "turns away his ear from hearing the law" is an "abomination." When we seek God in prayer but nowhere else, we miss the point. We show that we are far less interested in giving everything we can to the Lord than we are in getting what we desire.

We don't love God and others to get what we want. Prayer is one of the ways loyal people communicate with their Lord. As Moody notes, "The prayer of the humble and the contrite heart is a delight to God. There is no sound that goes up from this sin-cursed earth so sweet to His ear as the prayer of the man who is walking uprightly."[9] God delights in the prayers of those who devote their lives to him, and so we must pray within the context of a life that is "worthy of the gospel of Christ" (Phil. 1:27 ESV).

Surely, becoming a people of prayer will involve making prayer a central part of our lives. However, Dwight Moody pointed out that our prayers are not truly sincere or effective if we are neglecting the other aspects of the Christian life. He says that to become prayerful, we must commit to loving God and neighbor. We do not have to be perfect before coming to God in prayer because God is patient with our flaws. However, we should not think that because we pray, we need not attend to other aspects of our lives. God is not fooled by "those who call evil good and good evil" (Isa. 5:20 ESV) and continue to come to him in prayer. To be a people of prayer is to affirm the truth and to live in the light of it. We cannot allow prayer to take on the appearance of piety without the substance.

---

[9] Moody, *Prevailing Prayer*, 33.

THE MODEL PRAYER

When the disciples ask Jesus how to pray, he responds with what has become known as the Lord's Prayer (Luke 11:1–4). Many churches pray the Lord's prayer verbatim during their worship services, highlighting the prayer's emphasis on praying as a community of "us" and "we." The prayer itself offers insight into how we might pray in our own words. It points the way to the sort of prayers God's people should be offering. Each portion offers a unique opportunity for us to express ourselves in prayer.

Our Father, who art in heaven, hallowed be thy name…

Jesus begins by affirming God's position and seeking God's glory. He hallows God's name (Matt. 6:9–10). As professor and biblical scholar Craig Keener explains, "Jesus' prayer…yearns for the day when God's name alone will be hallowed, that is, sanctified or shown holy, special above every other name."[10] If we express our desire for God to be glorified as we begin to pray, we place God first above our own agendas.

Your kingdom come, your will be done, on earth as it is in heaven…

Jesus continues by affirming his desire to see the kingdom of God fully established. As we pray for God's kingdom to come, we affirm that the world around us is not as it should be. We express our longing for God to fix the broken world around us as only he can. We pray for the will of God to overcome the ways of the world.

Give us this day our daily bread…

Here Jesus does not ask for abundance or great wealth but for the needs of the day. While we can certainly ask for more than our daily needs, this portion of the prayer shows that we should pray in a way that keeps our

---

10 Craig S. Keener, *The Gospel of Matthew: A Socio-Rhetorical Commentary* (Grand Rapids: Eerdmans, 2009), 219.

selfish ambitions in check. When we pray that God would provide for our daily needs, we acknowledge that our lives are in God's hands and avoid the temptation to place our faith in the gifts rather than the Giver.

Forgive us our debts as we forgive our debtors…

Those who are unwilling to forgive will not be forgiven. In this section of the prayer, Jesus emphasizes the vital link between the debts we owe and the debts others owe to us. Those who are incapable of forgetting the debts owed to them demonstrate that they have not learned what it means to be forgiven because "If we do not learn to forgive then we will not be forgiven, we will not be part of the new reality, the new people, brought into existence by Jesus."[11] To be a forgiven people, we must be a forgiving people. While one does not cause the other, the two are inextricably intertwined with our willingness to forgive standing as a sign of our readiness to be forgiven.

And lead us not into temptation but deliver us from evil.

Finally, Jesus tells the disciples to pray that they would be delivered from the evil one. If we are praying for God's name to be glorified, it makes sense that we would also seek God's help in avoiding the sort of tests that would ultimately make us succumb to sin. By standing up to the tests of the evil one, God's people proclaimed the glory of God.

BECOMING PRAYERFUL

To become a praying people, then, we must learn to begin our prayers by expressing our desire for God to be glorified. This desire is exactly what Dwight Moody had in mind when he said, "Before we pray that God would fill us, I believe we ought to pray Him to empty us."[12]

11 C. F. D. Moule, *Essays in New Testament Interpretation* (Cambridge: Cambridge University Press, 1982), 282.
12 Moody, *Secret Power,* 32.

We certainly bring who we are to our prayers. We express our desires, concerns, and gratitude. Yet we do not pray for our own will to be done or for our names to be hallowed. When God empties us of our pride and misdirected desires, we will find ourselves ready to be filled with humility, compassion, and a yearning to see God glorified.

There is nothing in the Lord's prayer that reinforces our own "pride and selfishness and ambition and self-seeking."[13] Jesus is not giving us a secret formula to have our best life now. Instead, he offers us a paradigm for prayer that elevates God and his purposes above our own. Such is the nature of prayer. It arises not simply because we have wants or needs, however legitimate they may be, but because we have a deep, unyielding desire to see all that God has made glorify him.

---

13 Moody, *Secret Power*, 31.

WALK IN THE WORD

"The Lord makes poor and makes rich; he brings low and he exalts. He raises up the poor from the dust; he lifts the needy from the ash heap to make them sit with princes and inherit a seat of honor. For the pillars of the earth are the Lord's and on them he has set the world."

— *1 Samuel 2:7-8 ESV*

Hannah was barren. To make matters worse, her husband's other wife, Peninnah, had children and "used to provoke [Hannah] grievously to irritate her, because the Lord had closed [Hannah's] womb" (1 Sam. 1:6 ESV). Despite the kind treatment of her husband Elkanah, Hannah longed for a son. Ultimately, she vows that if God will give her a son, she will "give him to the Lord all the days of his life, and no razor shall touch his head" (1 Sam. 1:11 ESV).

God honored Hannah's request, and "in due time Hannah conceived and bore a son, and she called his name Samuel, for she said, 'I have asked for him from the Lord'" (1 Sam. 1:20 ESV). Hannah fulfills her vow and gives Samuel over to the Lord to serve in the temple at Shiloh (1 Sam. 1:26–28). She then offers a prayer that sets the stage for the rest of the books of 1 and 2 Samuel (1 Sam. 2:1–10).

Hannah's prayer is both an expression of praise and a theological interpretation of the events that will come to pass in the life of David and Israel. The prayer highlights the reversal of fortune that God so often brings about through his sovereign activities and for his glory. When no human options can address a problem, it is easy to recognize God's hand at work. Peninnah's fertility made it easier for her to forget God's blessing, but Hannah's barrenness was a constant reminder of her need for God. It inspired humility rather than pride.

Hannah's request for a son comes through her desperate prayer to the God who "watches over his holy ones" (1 Sam. 2:9 NET). Throughout Hannah's prayer in 1 Samuel 2, she emphasizes God's power manifested in the lives of those who live according to his will. Throughout our unsettled and tumultuous human affairs by which we often try to dethrone God, the Lord remains king over all. God suppresses the uprisings of those who would use the talents and position he bestowed on them for their own advancement. He exalts those who humbly follow him. God protects his people (1 Sam. 2:2, 9–10), orders the world (2:8), and judges humanity (2:4–8).

Hannah's prayers in the first two chapters of 1 Samuel remind us that when we pray, we pray to a God who has no limitations. He overcomes what is, for us, insurmountable. We pray to a God who will do great things in the lives of those who love him and commit to living according to his wisdom. He is the God who recognizes the humility and trust required to pray and to wait for God to answer our prayers.

Because Hannah was barren, we could say that prayer was her last resort and only option. Yet the point of the narrative is not to teach us that God will be there once we have exhausted all other options. Instead, it teaches us that God dwells in a higher realm beyond our own strength and understanding. We must embrace the truth that God "will guard the feet of his faithful ones, but the wicked shall be cut off in darkness, for not by might shall a man prevail" (1 Sam. 2:9 ESV). Only then will we see that we pray to a God who reverses fortunes and honors those who obey and depend on him.

REFLECTION QUESTIONS

01 | How central is prayer to your life? Does it occupy the margins, or do you have a lifestyle of prayer?

02 | Read Hannah's prayer in 1 Samuel 2. How would you describe God?

03 | Hannah's prayer of praise comes on the heels of an answered prayer. What does it look like to offer a prayer of praise when our prayers have not been answered?

04 | Hannah represents God well in her prayer. How can we misrepresent God through prayer? What sort of posture should we bring to prayer?

05 | What does your commitment to prayer (or lack thereof) say about you? What does the commitment (or lack thereof) of the body of Christ to prayer say about the church?

06 | How might we go about cultivating a life of prayer?

07 | Having read about this characteristic of Dwight L. Moody, how prayerful do you think you are?

08 | How can you change your life to be a more prayerful person as God wants you to be?

To move towards becoming more "prayerful," I will:

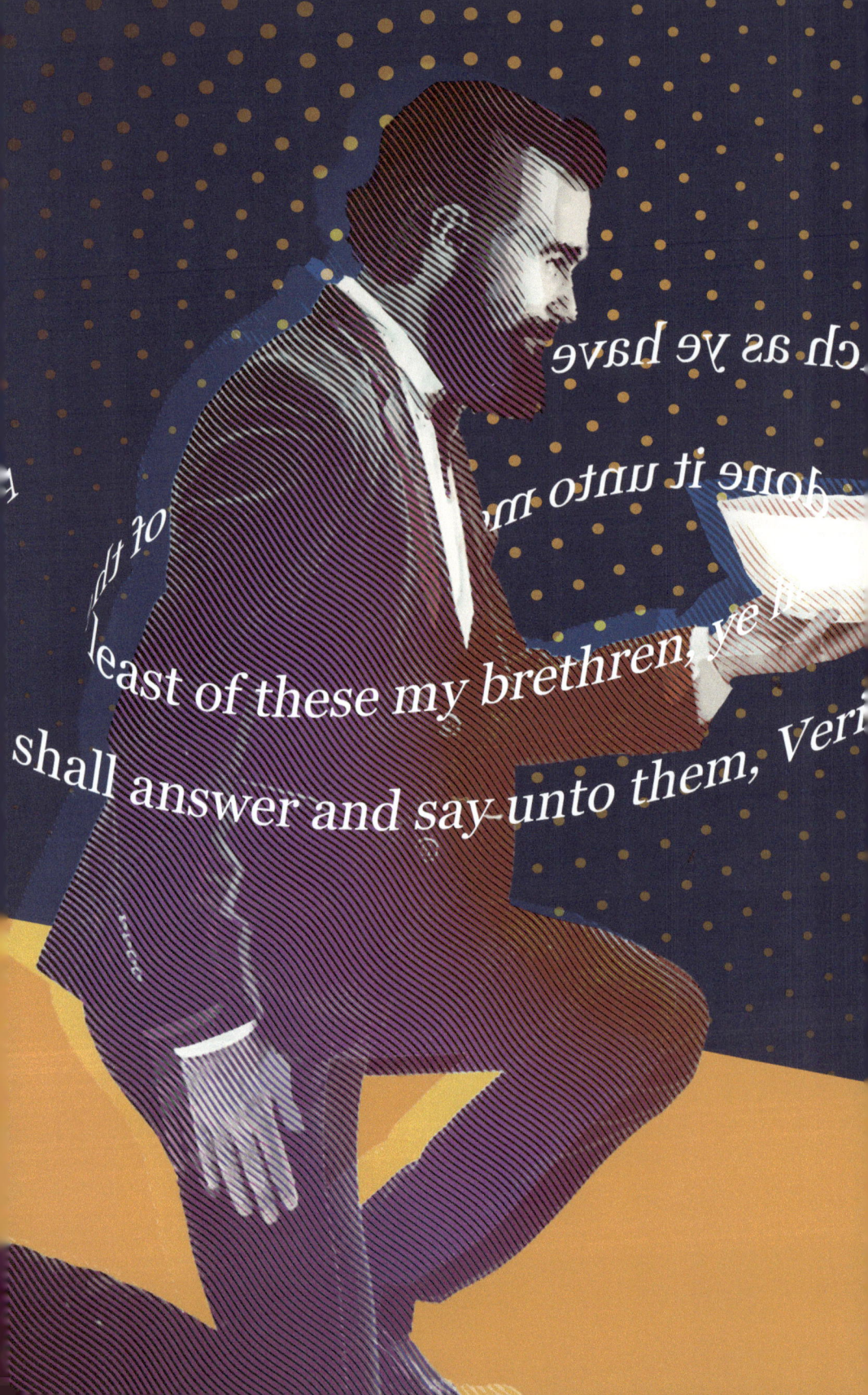

04

STUDIOUS

"Reading the Bible and remembering the poor—a combination of faith and works—will always bring joy."

– D. L. Moody,
Men of the Bible

Most people who know Dwight L. Moody do not regard him as an academician or a theologian but as one of the most effective evangelists in history. He lacked the formal education to be known as a scholar, but he was highly successful in his ministry. Yet if we view Moody primarily as an evangelist, we lose sight of the fact that Dwight Moody was a student of the Scriptures. He was a theologian, as all God's people are, because "To be a Christian theologian is to seek, speak, and show understanding of what God was doing in Christ for the sake of the world."[1]

With this description of a theologian in mind, we can begin to understand Moody as a theologian and a student of the scriptures. Dwight Moody was a lifelong student of the Scriptures. His thoughts about God's word led him not only to preach but also to live faithfully. He was an individual who dedicated himself to seeking, speaking, and showing his "understanding of what God was doing in Christ for the sake of the world."[2]

WORD AND WORK

Moody was a prolific speaker and writer, but his most profound theological work cannot be found in print. Instead, it is displayed in the life and continued influence of this man from Massachusetts who was overshadowed by God for the sake of the gospel. We don't regard Moody as an intellectual like C. S. Lewis or a pastor-theologian like Jonathan Edwards or A. W. Tozer. However, Moody's work was shaped by a keen, ongoing reading of the biblical text. As Moody himself notes, "Word and work make healthy Christians. If it be all Word and no work, people will suffer from what I may call religious gout. On the other hand, if it be all work and no Word, it will not be long before they will fall into all kinds of sin and error; so that they will do more harm than good."[3]

---

1 Kevin J. Vanhoozer and Owen Strachan, *The Pastor as Public Theologian: Reclaiming a Lost Vision* (Grand Rapids: Baker, 2015), 17.
2 Vanhoozer, *The Pastor as Public Theologian*, 17.
3 D. L. Moody, *Pleasure and Profit in Bible Study* (New York: Fleming H. Revell, 1895), 8.

When Moody speaks of the reciprocal relationship between the study of God's word and the work of the Christian life, he is hitting on an important concept: knowledge without discipleship is dangerous. Acquiring knowledge without learning to serve and obey will "contribute to what medieval thinkers regarded as the vice of *curiositas*, knowledge of important things lodged in minds unsuited to steward them."[4] To serve without a deep knowledge of God's word may lead us to invert the greatest commandment and the second, which is like it, so that love of neighbor becomes more important than love of God (Matt. 22:37–39).

Mr. Moody understood that knowing the Bible is not an end in itself, though he certainly viewed it as a task of paramount importance. At one point, he notes, "If I could say something that would induce Christians to have a deeper love for the Word of God, I should feel this to be the most important service that could be rendered to them."[5] We must develop a love for God's word. As we study, we should aim to become like the blessed one described in the first psalm whose "delight is in the law of the Lord, and on his law, he meditates day and night" (Ps. 1:2 ESV).

God reveals himself to us in the Scriptures. Studying the Bible but missing God makes our study an empty task. If we do not come to know God, we do not really understand the Scriptures we study. Through the study of God's word, we allow God to transform us so that we become a people capable of walking in "newness of life" (Rom. 6:4 ESV). As we allow the Bible to help us become more like Christ, our identity in Christ becomes the defining framework for our interactions with the world and each other. We recognize that Bible study is not an isolated intellectual task. While "many people have the Bible in their heads, or

---

[4] Thomas Albert Howard, *Protestant Theology and the Making of the Modern German University* (Oxford: Oxford University Press, 2006), 406.
[5] Moody, *Pleasure and Profit in Bible Study*, 7-8.

in their pockets," it is crucial that we get God's word "down into our hearts."[6] Such is what it means to be a student of the Scriptures.

THE BOOK AND THE BODY

In approaching the word of God, we do so as members of Christ's body. We each bring a particular perspective that influences the way we understand the Bible. Some of these perspectives will help us understand the biblical text more faithfully. Others will hinder us from doing so. We need the perspectives and expertise of others to fill in the gaps and reveal our blind spots.

As we study, we remain humble while utilizing our unique skills and capacities. Humility does not mean that we deny the church of our God-given talents. We remain aware of our unique potential to contribute despite our limitations. We work diligently to understand the Scriptures, not for fame and fortune but to glorify God by contributing to the body of Christ as we seek the mutual encouragement that comes from life in community (Rom. 1:11–12).

Bible study is not an isolated activity but one done in conversation with other believers. Looking to the community of faith is not a sign of weakness. It is a recognition that we are people of the book and the body. As Dwight Moody notes, "I would advise all your converts to keep as much as they can in the company of more experienced Christians. I like to keep in the society of those who know more than I do, and I never lose a chance of getting all the good I can out of them."[7]

---

6 D. L. Moody, *Short Talks* (Chicago: The Bible Institute Colportage Association, 1900), 103.
7 Moody, *Pleasure and Profit* in Bible Study, 9.

BECOMING A STUDENT OF GOD'S WORD

STEP 1: PREPARE TO STUDY.

When we devote ourselves to study, we prepare ourselves to contribute well to the body of Christ through the study of God's word. Unfortunately, we live in a world that seeks to shape us into its image. It can be tempting for us to adopt the ways of the world rather than allowing God's word to be "a lamp for my feet, a light on my path" (Ps. 119:105 NIV). In studying God's word, we seek to resist the allure of charting our own course or placing our trust in the world's judgments. If we deny ourselves the blessings of knowing God's word, we leave ourselves open to formative influences of other sorts.

On the other hand, if we immerse ourselves in the Scriptures, we can embrace what it means to be the right kind of strange in a fallen world. The Scriptures call us to move from darkness to light. They teach us to move and think differently in the world. We study, knowing that "God gives us his word and Spirit not simply to inform but to form and transform, to renew our knowledge and refresh our love for God (Rom. 12:2); to cultivate not only new thoughts but habits of thought, a way of thinking in accordance with the gospel."[8]

It is through the study of the Scriptures that we learn to resist temptation, especially temptation which "consists not so much in the titanic desire to be as God, but in weakness, timidity, weariness, not wanting to be what God requires of us."[9] Through the study of the Bible, we learn to see with Christian eyes and hear with Christian ears as we look out upon the world

---

[8] Kevin J. Vanhoozer and Daniel J. Treier, *Theology and the Mirror of Scripture: A Mere Evangelical Account* (Downers Grove: InterVarsity, 2015), 99.

[9] Jürgen Moltmann, *Theology of Hope: On the Ground and the Implications of a Christian Eschatology* (Minneapolis: Fortress, 1993), 22.

in light of God's presence. In study, we prepare ourselves to be citizens of God's kingdom and to walk according to his ways.

STEP 2: APPROACH GOD'S WORD WELL.

Second, to become a student of God's word, we need to consider how we approach God's word. There is certainly something to be said for reading the whole Bible, yet we do not want to be like those who "skim along so quickly that they see nothing."[10] Instead, we should read the Scriptures as if we are "seeking for something of value. It is a good deal better to take a single chapter and spend a month on it than to read the Bible at random for a month."[11] God's word demands our consistent time and attention if we are to develop a love for it. We cannot expect to love something that is relegated to the margins of our day.

In addition, as we approach God's word, we must do so expecting to be changed. There is a way for us to study the Scriptures to authorize our own thoughts and perspectives. It is possible for us to read the Scriptures selectively to avoid the parts that might challenge our agendas and force us to redirect our misdirected desires. As Bonhoeffer noted in a lecture given at the Ecumenical Conference at Gland, "Has it not become terrifyingly clear again and again, in everything that we have said here to one another, that we are no longer obedient to the Bible? We are more fond of our own thoughts than of the thoughts of the Bible. We no longer read the Bible seriously, we no longer read it against ourselves, but for ourselves."[12]

To prefer our thoughts to the thoughts of the Bible is to set aside the wisdom of God. We must approach the Bible with a willingness to have our eyes opened that we may see and our hearing enhanced so that we may listen. We do not have the option of picking and choosing the parts of the Bible we choose to obey. Instead, we must "cling to the whole

---

10 Moody, *Pleasure and Profit in Bible Study*, 52.
11 Moody, *Pleasure and Profit in Bible Study*, 47.
12 Dietrich Bonhoeffer, *No Rusty Swords: Letters, Lectures and Notes, 1928-1936*, from the *Collected Works of Dietrich Bonhoeffer*, Volume 1 (New York: Harper and Row, 1965), 185-18.

Bible, not a part of it. A man is not going to do much with a broken sword."[13]

STEP 3: DEVOTE TIME FOR STUDY.

Finally, to become a student of God's word, we must set aside time to spend in study. Those who "have neglected the Word of God" and "neglected to care for the new life, will sink into weakness and decay, and [are] easily stumbled or offended."[14] When we allow other influences and distractions to crowd out or devalue God's word, we can be sure that we have allowed the urgencies of the day to keep us from sitting at the feet of Jesus. We must devote time to deep study of God's word. We need the time to "be still" and know that God is God (Ps. 46:10). Our willingness to set aside whatever other matters place demands on our time to study the Scriptures demonstrates our conviction that God's word is a lamp to our feet and a light to our path (Ps. 119:105).

In his fictional account of a dystopian future in *Brave New World*, Aldous Huxley notes that we have developed "a vast mass communications industry concerned in the main neither with the true nor the false, but with the unreal, the more or less totally irrelevant."[15] He says that those who develop these systems "failed to take into account man's almost infinite appetite for distractions."[16] Distractions are dangerous for us if our aim is to find delight in God's instruction. Distractions compete with God's word for our time and attention. They tell tales devoid of God and therefore devoid of hope. They trivialize life by marginalizing God and his place in the world. Yet if we are to be useful to God, we would do well to embrace Paul's instruction to Timothy: "Be diligent to present yourself approved to God as a worker who does not need to be ashamed, accurately handling the word of truth" (2 Tim. 2:15 NASB).

---

13 Dwight L. Moody as quoted in the *Official Report of the Eleventh International Christian Endeavor Convention* (Boston: United Society of Christian Endeavor, 1892), 144.
14 Moody, *Pleasure and Profit in Bible Study*, 13.
15 Aldous Huxley, *Brave New World and Brave New World Revisited* (New York: Harper Perennial Modern Classics, 2005), 267.
16 Huxley, *Brave New World and Brave New World Revisited*, 267.

WALK IN THE WORD

"Blessed is the man who walks not in the counsel of the wicked, nor stands in the way of sinners, nor sits in the seat of scoffers; but his delight is in the law of the Lord, and on his law he meditates day and night.

He is like a tree planted by streams of water that yields its fruit in its season, and its leaf does not wither. In all he does, he prospers."

– Psalm 1:1-3 ESV

Standing on the border of the Promised Land, Moses reminds the Israelites of the importance of God's commands. God has given Israel a gift. He tells them how to live in the world under his sovereign, wise, and benevolent rule. He wants to immerse them in God's instruction until it permeates Israel's life. As Moses says,

> And these words that I command you today shall be on your heart. You shall teach them diligently to your children and shall talk of them when you sit in your house, and when you walk by the way, and when you lie down, and when you rise. You shall bind them as a sign on your hand, and they shall be as frontlets between your eyes. You shall write them on the doorposts of your house and on your gates (Deut. 6:6-9 ESV).

God's instruction offers to shape the life of his people. Through his instruction, Israel could learn the wisdom of obedience by following God's instruction rather than walking "in the counsel of the wicked" (Ps. 1:1 ESV). It was through obedience that Israel demonstrated their loyalty to God. Obedience was to bring blessing (Deut. 11:13-14; 12:28; 28:1). Delighting in God's instruction promises nourishment (Ps. 1:3).

It is possible to think of God's law, or even the Old Testament as a whole, as strange, unnecessary, or outdated. But such a perspective prevents us from knowing God more deeply. If we set aside the Old Testament, we will lose the opportunity to benefit from the full counsel of God's word (Acts 20:27). We might say the same for the New Testament. The scriptures of the Old and New Testaments reveal who God is and offer opportunities for us to be taught, reproved, corrected, and trained in righteousness (2 Tim 3:16).

As people who are to be and make disciples, we are to teach others all that Jesus commanded (Matt. 28:19-20). We are to show our love for God by obeying his commandments (1 John 5:2). We are to "destroy arguments and every lofty opinion raised against the knowledge of God and take every thought captive to obey Christ" (2 Cor. 10:5 ESV). It is through God's word that we learn wisdom and come to understand that our plans are, at best, provisional because we "do not know what tomorrow will bring" (James 4:14 ESV).

Learning to delight in God's law is not simply a matter of memorization or constant study. We are to be practical students of the word who delight in study but also put God's word into practice. In part, we delight in study because through it, we learn to see the world as God's creation, the space in which he continues to rule and act. We also delight in God's word because as we obey it, we are better able to recognize all that God is doing in the world. To delight in God's instruction is to obey. And to obey is to place our trust in God to care for us even when we don't understand how he will do so.

REFLECTION QUESTIONS

01 | How might you go about cultivating a delight of God's instruction?

02 | Why does delighting in God's word keep us from taking counsel from the wicked?

03 | How have you arranged your life to immerse yourself in God's instruction?

04 | How do you take every thought captive to Christ (2 Cor 10:5)?

05 | In what ways can we faithfully teach others all that Christ has commanded?

06 | How can we become more studious?

07 | Having read about this characteristic of Dwight L. Moody, how studious do you think you are?

08 | What do you think you need to change about the way you live to become more studious?

To move towards becoming more "studious," I will:

05

HUMBLE

"We are nothing, but Christ is everything, and what we want is to keep in communion with Him and let Christ dwell in us richly and shine forth through us."

— D. L. Moody,
Moody's Stories

After bringing multiple plagues upon the Egyptians, God sends Moses and Aaron to Pharaoh to ask a simple question: "How long will you refuse to humble yourself before me?" (Exod. 10:3 ESV). Pharaoh's stubbornness and hardness of heart kept him from yielding to God's obvious power and authority. Even though God had demonstrated his might through the plagues, Pharaoh continues to resist God. Ironically, Pharaoh's unwillingness to humble himself is exactly what God wants Israel to avoid once they are set free from the Egyptian ruler.

In Deuteronomy 8:16 (NASB), Moses reflects on God's history with his people noting, "In the wilderness He fed you manna which your fathers did not know, that He might humble you and that He might test you, to do good for you in the end." God does not seek to humble Israel in the sense that he afflicts or defeats them (cf. Deut. 21:14; 2 Sam. 8:1; 1 Chron. 17:10; Ps. 81:15). Instead, he desires to remind them of his position in relation to them. They need to recognize their limitations and learn to trust and obey the Lord.

Humility is a virtue espoused throughout the scriptures. Moses's humility stands in contrast to the self-serving assertions of Miriam and Aaron in Numbers 12:1–16. Ahab is spared disaster and devastation in his lifetime because he humbled himself before the Lord (1 Kings 21:29). God is often pictured as standing with the humble (1 Sam. 2:7; Ps. 10:17; 37:11; 75:1; Prov. 11:2; 16:19; 29:23; Matt. 18:4; James 4:10). Jesus humbled himself in the incarnation (Phil. 2:5-7), and in doing so, demonstrates that self-giving sacrifice is part of "what equality with God meant in practice."[1] Christ did not view his equality with God "as excusing him from the task of (redemptive) suffering and death, but actually as uniquely qualifying him for that vocation."[2] As such, God "will recognize self-giving love in his people as the true mark of the life

---

1 N. T. Wright, *The Climax of the Covenant: Christ and the Law in Pauline Theology* (Minneapolis: Fortress, 1993), 87.
2 Wright, *The Climax of the Covenant*, 84.

of the Spirit. Christ's own example is held up for the church to imitate; not that his incarnation, death, and exaltation are merely exemplary, but they are at least that."3

IMPORTANCE OF HUMILITY

Humility is our way of orienting truthfully to the world. When we practice humility, we do not project a false perception of ourselves. Instead, like Christ, we humble ourselves because we understand what it means to be truly human. Humans are limited. We all have shortcomings. To be human is to have vulnerabilities. As theologian Stanley Hauerwas suggests, "Humility determined by truthfulness makes possible the acknowledgment of our defects and faults without exaggerating those defects and faults."4

The connection between humility and the truth is an important one if we wish to avoid being overly or falsely humble. Humility does not deny our God-given strengths, talents, and achievements. Instead, it recognizes that God is the source of all we have. It means we acknowledge that our strength comes from the Lord. Therefore, we operate with a humble strength. We are strong because, in Christ, we have become victors. We are humble because we know that even our most impressive attributes were given to us by God for his use. We are not self-made women and men. We are creatures intended to reflect God to the world.

Despite (and often because of) our obvious shortcomings, God uses us to accomplish his purposes. Working through us to do things that we could never accomplish demonstrates God's power. Such achievements point beyond us. However, it is still easy for us to believe that we accomplish everything ourselves through the strength of our hands (Deut. 8:17).

---

3 Wright, *The Climax of the Covenant*, 87.
4 Stanley Hauerwas, *The Work of Theology* (Grand Rapids: Eerdmans, 2015), 164.

Commenting on John the Baptist, Dwight Moody observed, "If we preached down ourselves and exalted Christ, the world would soon be reached. The world is perishing today for the want of Christ. The church could do without our theories and pet views, but not without Christ."[5] Moody goes on to note that if the church and its leaders would "get behind the cross, so that Christ is held up, the people will come flocking to hear the Gospel."[6] He understood that without proper humility derived from the grace of God, the church would set itself on a pedestal and mask God from the world.

Rather than revel in his own accomplishments, Moody understood the paradoxical nature of the Christian life: God works through "foolish things, weak things, base things, despised things and things which are not."[7] As he notes, "When we are weak, then we are strong. People often think they have not strength enough; the fact is we have too much strength. It is when we feel that we have no strength of our own that we are willing God should use us, and work through us. If we are leaning on God's strength, we have more than all the strength of the world."[8] Such is the nature of humility. We recognize our utter need for God, wait for his strength and guidance to act, and attribute all glory to him. After all, "No matter how weak you are, God can use you; and you cannot say what a stream of salvation you may set in motion."[9]

Moody was convinced that God would use "men and women of average talent" to reach the world.[10] This perspective is somewhat lost on the church today as we look toward those with great talent or wealth to lead in ministry. We have not always imitated God in exalting the humble or being impartial. So, "whatever gifts or talents you have, take and lay

---

5 D. L. Moody, *Bible Characters* (Chicago: Fleming H. Revell, 1888), 119.
6 Moody, *Bible Characters*, 119.
7 Moody, *To the Work! To the Work!*, 65.
8 Moody, *To the Work! To the Work!*, 65-66.
9 Moody, *Pleasure and Profit in Bible Study*, 114.
10 Moody, *To the Work! To the Work!*, 69.

them at the Master's feet" because God "will link His mighty power with our weakness, and we shall be able to do great things for Him."[11] God is not searching for those who can do great things on their own but for those who are open to God doing great things through them.

MOODY'S MODEL OF HUMILITY

Moody's early life and lack of formal education may have helped him understand humility. However, his global notoriety as an evangelist and his success in his later years could easily have made being humble a challenge. He was the most influential preacher of his day and saw multiple millions come to Christ through his evangelistic campaigns. He built many schools to educate women and men to be useful for God. Yet, Moody frequently shunned the limelight, even declining to give permission to have his picture printed in papers. In a letter from D. L. Moody's wife Emma to Harpers Brothers declining permission to print a picture of Mr. Moody, she writes, "…I am glad he does not care for this sort of prominence. I wish very much that so much need not be said of workers for Christ."[12] May we all seek to be overshadowed so that Christ may be glorified.

In his book about Moody, R. A. Torrey writes, "…he was the most humble man I ever knew, i.e., the most humble man when we bear in mind the great things he did, and the praise that was lavished upon him."[13] Moody had sufficient reach and reputation to preach wherever and whenever he wanted. He could easily have become the headline in any setting, leaving Christ behind. However, Moody remained steadfast to God and sought to stay in the background so that Christ took center stage.

---

11 Moody, *To the Work! To the Work!*, 71.
12 Emma Moody to Robert R. McBurney, 1885, YMCA Collection, D. L. Moody Center Digital Archives, https://archives.moodycenter.org/digital/collection/p17348coll5/id/1/rec/3
13 Torrey, *Why God Used D. L. Moody*, 28.

At times, Moody recognized that his notoriety got in the way of his message. In 1896, Moody was invited to preach in New York but did not immediately accept the invitation. His concern was that he would have difficulty reaching non-churchgoers there. He anticipated that once church members heard he was coming, they would fill the hall, leaving no room for the lost. Moody attributed this problem to his reputation noting, "Reputation is a great injury in many places, for we cannot get the people that we are after."[14] Moody's perspective on the New York trip illustrates his desire to stand behind Christ. He was not looking to build himself up by filling halls with his admirers but to proclaim Christ to those who most needed to hear his message most.

We also see Moody's humility in his day-to-day dealings with the church. In a letter to his brother George Moody, the evangelist advises about some tensions that threaten to create disunity in the church. After expressing his concerns about the YMCA, which he does not describe in detail, Moody urges George to do what is needed to preserve peace in the body of Christ. He encourages George to "take a back seat" if that will ensure peace. Moody's willingness to privilege the good of the church over the power of man rather than elevate himself or his family's interests over that of the body of Christ demonstrates his own personal humility.

He urges George to step away from leadership opportunities for the sake of unity, writing, "…if there is any feeling against the Moodys, do not let the church get down on us. Let us take a back seat and will come all right in the course of time, but you see what a fearful thing it would be to have a division just at this time and you must do all you can to keep peace."[15] In taking a back seat, Moody recognizes that holding a particular leadership position is less crucial than the ongoing unity of the body.

---

14 William R. Moody, *The Life of Dwight L. Moody* (Amsterdam: Fredonia, 2001), 315.
15 D. L. Moody to George Moody, 1879, TMC Collection, D. L. Moody Center Digital Archives, https://archives.moodycenter.org/digital/collection/p17348coll1/id/423/rec/4

While there are numerous examples of humility throughout the life and work of D. L. Moody, there is perhaps no better illustration of it than his willingness to publicly repent. His son, William, describes a time after an evangelistic meeting when a man in attendance insulted Moody. Letting his temper get the best of him, "Instantly [Dwight Moody] thrust the man from him and sent him reeling down the remaining steps to the vestibule."[16] As Moody stood up to begin the evangelistic meeting, he apologized for giving way to his temper and asked for everyone's forgiveness. William noted the impression of one of Moody's friends who was in attendance, who said, "There was not a word of excuse or vindication for resenting the insult. The impression made by his words was wonderful, and instead of the meeting being killed by the scene it was greatly blessed by such a consistent and straight-forward confession."[17]

Surely, we could look back at Moody's apology with cynical eyes and conclude that he had no choice but to repent; there were too many witnesses to ignore what had happened. Yet, there are simply too many reports of Moody's life and character to assume that his humility was not at work. When Moody asked for forgiveness, he demonstrated the humility that confession requires. To live in truth is often inconvenient. When we repent, we admit that we have done something wrong. Such an admission is both a beautiful act of humility and a moment when we can clearly proclaim God's grace.

---

16 Moody, *The Life of Dwight L. Moody*, 110
17 Moody, *The Life of Dwight L. Moody*, 111.

HOW TO DEVELOP HUMILITY

STEP 1: ACCEPT YOURSELF AS GOD'S CREATION.

To be humble, we must first embrace our identity as created beings made in the image of a sovereign, benevolent, wise, and holy God. God has created us to reflect his glory to the world. He has gifted us with (a) others, (b) our unique abilities and perspectives, and (c) our (now fallen) world. These gifts are not to be wasted on self-centered pursuits. Instead, they remind us that all we are and all we have is from the Lord. God's gifts should not cultivate pride. They should humble us and make us thankful.

God places each of us within the body of Christ so that we may contribute to the building up of the church. Our God-given gifts may mean we are suited to play a particular role within the body, but no role in the body is more important than another. It is up to us to accept our role humbly and joyfully as members of Christ's body. We must resist using who we are and what we have for our own advantage. Like Christ, we must humble ourselves, not just by giving up equality with God but by allowing all we are and all we have to be directed towards the work he has given us to do.

STEP 2: RECOGNIZE OTHERS.

Humility requires that we recognize the contributions others make in our lives. In Romans 1:11–12 (NIV), Paul highlights the mutuality that exists within the body of Christ: "I long to see you so that I may impart to you some spiritual gift to make you strong—that is, that you and I may be mutually encouraged by each other's faith." Here, we see that Paul does not deny the contribution he will certainly make in Rome. Instead, he assumes that his own contribution will be matched by the body of Christ in Rome. Humility keeps Paul from assuming that, as an apostle, he has nothing to learn from anyone else. In the same way, to be humble is to recognize that we are incomplete and need the other members of the church and their God-given gifts.

STEP 3: SHARE OUR GIFTS.

Finally, humility demands self-giving. We must believe that the gifts we have been given are not to be used solely for our benefit. We don't have to deprive ourselves at every turn, but we must remember Christ's example. He did not see equality with God as something to be used for his own benefit but for our benefit (Phil. 2:5-11). We must have an eye toward others. When we do, we will be willing to humble ourselves regardless of our position in society, our gifts, and our talents.

WALK IN THE WORD

> "Be devoted to one another with mutual love, showing eagerness in honoring one another"

— *Romans 12:10 NET*

The Apostle Paul's letters contain rich theological insights regarding justification, sanctification, and the church. They are all worthy of our attention, as is every amazing act of love and redemption God performs. We were not saved by grace through faith to go on living however we choose (Eph. 2:8). Since our works can never make us righteous before our holy and just God, we must adopt a spirit of humility. We must recognize that our only reason for boasting is "in the cross of our Lord Jesus Christ" (Gal. 6:14 ESV).

In Romans 12, Paul reminds the community to love one another. After reminding the Jews and Gentiles that they have been justified by faith and united in Christ, Paul tells the believers in Rome to be humble: "For by the grace given to me I say to every one of you not to think more highly of yourself than you ought to think but to think with sober discernment, as God has distributed to each of you a measure of faith" (Rom. 12:3 NET). He goes on to remind those in the Roman church that "we who are many are one body in Christ, and individually we are members who belong to one another" (Rom. 12:5 NET). As we exercise our gifts within the community of faith, we do so without arrogance and without diminishing those who have other gifts.

Our talents do not exist in a hierarchy as if one gift is superior to another or one role in the church more important. The members of the body must all work together for the glory of God. Each member contributes. Each member matters. In 1 Corinthians, Paul writes, "The eye cannot say to the hand, 'I do not need you,' nor in turn can the head say to the foot, 'I do not need you'" (1 Cor. 12:21 NET). He goes on to note,

> God has blended together the body, giving greater honor to the lesser member, so that there may be no division of the body, but the members may have mutual concern for one another. If one

> member suffers, everyone suffers with it. If a member is honored, all rejoice with it (1 Cor. 12:24–26 NET).

To be humble does not mean that we set aside the gifts God has given us. Humility affirms in word and deed our need for other members of the body of Christ so that we are not "motivated by selfish ambition or vanity" but "in humility…treat one another as more important" than ourselves (Phil. 2:3 NET). It seeks to honor others even when it means setting aside our rights or preferences. It means that we "associate with the lowly" (Rom. 12:16 ESV) and practice "correcting opponents with gentleness" (2 Tim. 2:24 NET).

Having a spirit of humility is part of what it means to "live worthily of the calling with which you have been called" (Eph. 4:1 NET). We are humble knowing that we have no grounds for asserting our own virtues when any true wisdom we have about the world comes from God, any abilities or strengths are gifts from the Lord, any position we occupy is God-ordained, and any good works we accomplish are powered by the Holy Spirit. We do not seek to claim that we have earned the gifts God has given us, nor do we use them for our own advantage. Instead, as creatures beholden to our Creator for our very existence, we stand with humility before our Maker and amidst the rest of his creation, acknowledging all that he has given and seeking to look beyond our own interests to see the interests of others (Phil. 2:4).

REFLECTION QUESTIONS

01 Read Exod. 10:3; Deut. 8:2–3, 11–20; 2 Sam. 22:28; 2 Chron. 12:1–16; Pro. 15:33, 18:12, 22:4; Zeph. 2:3; Acts 20:19; Eph. 4:1–2; Phil. 2:1–11; Col 3:12; 1 Pt. 5:5. How would you describe humility in biblical perspective?

02 What are some of the ways that humility opens us up to be used by God?

03 How does humility look within the body of Christ?

04 Christ did not see his equality with God as something to be used for his own advantage (Phil. 2:6). How can you ensure that you are not simply using the gifts God has given you for your own advantage?

05 If humility is the opposite of pride, can you name some areas in your life where the temptation to be prideful rather than humble is a challenge?

06 How might learning more about God inspire humility?

07 | Having read about this characteristic of Dwight L. Moody, how would you describe your humility?

08 | What would have to change in your life for you to become a humbler person?

To move towards becoming more "humble," I will:

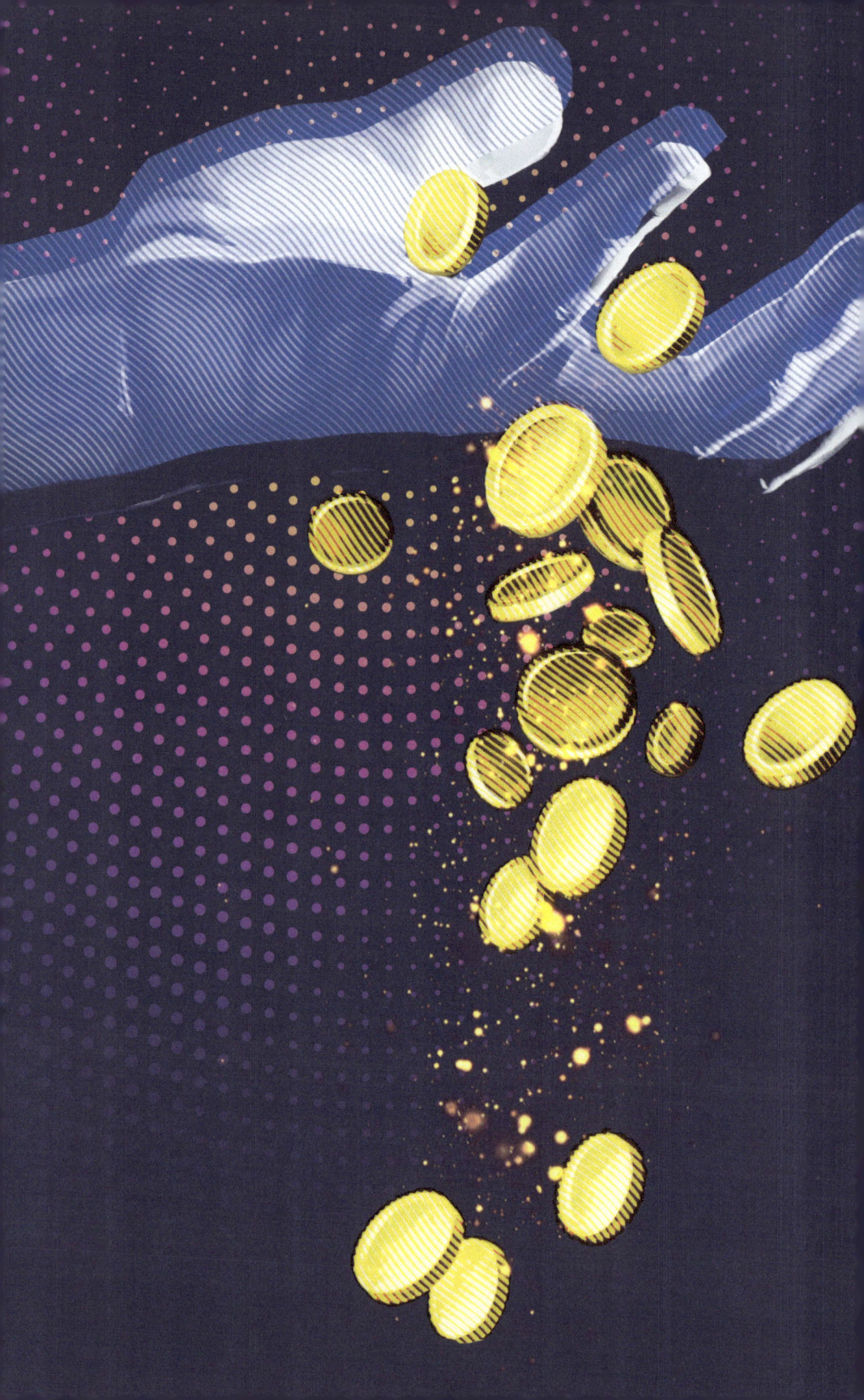

06
FREE FROM LOVE OF MONEY

> "The trouble nowadays is that it doesn't mean anything to some people to be a Christian. What we must have is a higher type of Christianity in this country. We must have a Christianity that has in it the principle of self-denial.
>
> We must deny ourselves. If we want power, we must be separate."
>
> – D. L. Moody,
> *Men of the Bible*

Our capitalist economy encourages us to pursue money and to think about the economy in a way that can easily transform us into men and women living as perfect consumers rather than as the image of Christ. Often, we don't even notice how much we are influenced by money and the logic of our economic systems. We have cities that celebrate capitalism. Perhaps none is more prominent than Las Vegas, which "is often described as a city of dreams and fantasy, of tinselish make-believe. But this is getting it backward. Vegas is instead the American market ethic stripped completely bare, a mini-world totally free of the pretenses and protocols of modern consumer capitalism."[1] When we lose sight of the theological truth that "man does not live by bread alone, but man lives by every word that comes from the mouth of the Lord," we will struggle to disentangle our lives from the allure of money (Deut. 8:3).

In William Moody's biography of his father, William reflects on one of the few times Dwight Moody responded publicly to a newspaper report. According to William, the press had suggested that Moody was "making a good thing financially out of his religious work."[2] William notes that with "tears in his eyes" and a quivering voice Dwight Moody offered the following response:

> As I know my heart, before God, I have never let the desire for money determine my conduct in any way. I know I am weak and come short in many ways, but the devil has not that hold upon me. I have never profited personally by a single dollar that has been raised through my work, and it hurts me to be charged with it, above all things. May God forgive those who say this of me.[3]

Moody, both by his own testimony and the testimony of others, was free from the love of money. As Dorsett suggests, the Moody family was

---
1 Marc Cooper, *The Last Honest Place in America: Paradise and Perdition in the New Las Vegas* (New York: Nation, 2004), 10.
2 Moody, *The Life of D. L. Moody*, 423.
3 Moody, *The Life of D. L. Moody*, 424.

never in need financially, yet "because Moody never solicited money for himself, and because of his generosity with what came into his hands, he escaped the horrid publicity and scandals that rocked later evangelists."[4] It is as Torrey said in his book: "Millions of dollars passed into Mr. Moody's hands, but they passed through; they did not stick to his fingers."[5]

MOODY AND MONEY

Moody was no lover of money. He understood the depths of God's fathomless generosity to those who dedicate themselves to him. He also recognized the dangers that a love of money posed to the life and ministry of God's people. Commenting on the challenges money can bring to Christian families, Moody notes,

> ...if we are doing anything in any business that is dishonorable in order to make money for our children, better a thousand times for us to leave them a clean record, a clean character, than to leave them millions of money that we have not gotten honestly.[6]

Moody also recognized that love for money requires a trade. We can't bet on the riches of the world and expect to receive the power of God. The riches of the world will always let us down. They are finite and fickle. As fleeting as money may be, if we give ourselves over to it, we will find that we cannot obey God fully. When our allegiance lies with worldly wealth, we cannot expect to love God with all we are and with all we have.

The love of money detaches us from the peace and possibilities God provides. Money is not a kind master. It makes demands, creates instability, and makes us slaves to our wants. Loving money is not like loving God because money does not offer blessing. Money steals our lives by enslaving us to our own misdirected desires.

---

4 Lyle W. Dorsett, *A Passion for Souls: The Life of D. L. Moody* (Chicago: Moody, 2003), 228.
5 Torrey, *Why God Used D. L. Moody*, 36.
6 D. L. Moody, *Bible Characters* (Chicago: Fleming, 1888), 89.

GREED AND LOVING MONEY

Greed is not good. It is insatiable. It leads us astray with its many promises but is incapable of satisfying our desires. Greed directs our desires away from God. When greed becomes our way of being in the world, it becomes easy to forget that God provides.

Greed is grounded in wanting rather than in obtaining. Whatever we get will not satisfy. It will only lead to wanting more. As the theologian Augustine notes, "…we call the greedy poor, who are always craving and always wanting. For they may possess ever so great an amount of money; but whatever be the abundance of that they are not able but to want."[7]

In connecting greed with idolatry, Paul highlights the true danger greed poses. It creates a screen between us and God. It fools us into thinking that it can provide security and satisfaction when only God can. When we succumb to greed, we risk experiencing an endless, hopeless life of insecurity. We are endlessly compelled to accumulate a surplus of wealth. Greed finds fertile ground in those without a deep knowledge of and belief in the sovereign, wise, benevolent Creator.

Greed also keeps us from reflecting God's glory to the world. Our desire for more money dominates us. It becomes the central focus of our lives so that we reflect the reigning economic logic of our day rather than the glory of God. As biblical scholar G. K. Beale notes in his book, *We Become What We Worship: A Biblical Theology of Idolatry*,

> …all humans have been created to be reflecting beings, and they will reflect whatever they are ultimately committed to, whether the true God or some other object in the created order. Thus, to repeat the primary theme of this book, we resemble what we revere, either for ruin or restoration.[8]

---

7 Saint Augustine, *The City of God*, trans. Marcus Dods (Peabody: Hendrickson, 2009), 196.
8 G. K. Beale, *We Become What We Worship: A Biblical Theology of Idolatry* (Downers Grove: InterVarsity, 2008), 22.

When we embrace greed, we worship a god of our own making. We end up serving our own needs rather than serving our Creator.

The people of biblical times faced the same challenge. In Luke 16, the Pharisees are portrayed as those "who loved money" (Luke 16:14 NIV). When they taught, it was unclear whether they were teaching to proclaim the truth or to proclaim the "truth" determined by the highest bidder. Labeling someone as a "money lover" in the ancient world was not a compliment. It was a common way to identify false teachers. "Money lovers" were unconcerned with the truth. They were not interested in benefiting society at large. They taught what would advance their own cause regardless of whether what they taught was true or not. Money lovers were willing to use their reputation and standing as an influencer for their own gain and with no regard for anyone else.

In other Greek literature, "money lovers" were often associated with idolatry and, most relevant for a reading of Luke 16:18, adultery. "Money lovers" were not simply greedy. They were individuals who sold out. They traded all that was righteous for all that was unrighteous to serve wealth rather than God.[9]

Dwight Moody did not give his heart to money. He understood its relative value. It isn't that money has no value but that its value is limited and unworthy of our devotion. For instance, in a letter of congratulations to an acquaintance named Thomas Coyle, Moody addresses Coyle's good reputation, saying, "Remember that you are making a name for yourself, and the Bible says a good name is better than ointment, is rather to be chosen than great riches."[10]

He also recognized the connection between money and the church's witness. Those who oppose the gospel can easily accuse people in

---

9 Robert C. Tannehill, *Luke* (Nashville: Abingdon, 1996), 249-250.
10 D. L. Moody to Thomas Coyle, 1884, Yale Collection, D. L. Moody Center Digital Archives, https://archives.moodycenter.org/digital/collection/p17348coll1/id/1651/rec/1

ministry of being "money lovers." Moody believed church leaders could keep these accusations at bay by expressing self-giving love and service to their neighbors. He notes,

> Do you want to know how you can reach the masses? Go to their homes and enter into sympathy with them; tell them you have come to do them good and let them see that you have a heart to feel for them. When they find out that you really love them, all those things that are in their hearts against Christianity will be swept out of the way. Atheists may tell them that you only want to get their money, and that you do not really care for their happiness. We have to contradict that lie by our lives and send it back to the pit where it came from.[11]

Loving money is an obstacle to selflessness because it assumes that every action must have a return. Christians allow God to direct their lives whether we are likely to receive a return or not. Rather than hoarding temporal goods, we look beyond the perishable to the imperishable. We adopt the perspective of Paul, who writes, "What is more, I consider everything a loss because of the surpassing worth of knowing Christ Jesus my Lord, for whose sake I have lost all things. I consider them garbage, that I may gain Christ" (Phil. 3:8 NIV).

So, how do we avoid being lovers of money?

---

11 Moody, *To the Work! To the Work!*, 97.

LOVING MONEY NO MORE

STEP 1: **DEVELOP GRATITUDE.**

First, we must learn to be grateful for all that we have. Gratitude is more than a passing expression of thanks. It is an affirmation that we understand the source of our wealth. Gratitude reminds us that God is the giver of all good gifts. As we give thanks to God for our resources, we affirm that God has given us all we have so that we might glorify him. In giving thanks to God for what we have, we would also do well to give thanks to God for allowing us to participate in all that he is doing in the world.

STEP 2: **THINK THEOLOGICALLY.**

Second, we must learn to reason theologically. As we cultivate a heart of gratitude, we begin to see the various ways the world ignores God and creates elaborate systems that oppose his ways. If we are not careful, we can develop attitudes towards money that are formed less by the Scriptures and more by the economic logic of the day. More money is better than less. A big ministry is better than a small one. The ends justify the means. Those with money are better than those without. Such ideas oppose biblical injunctions against partiality (Lev. 19:15; James 2:1–7), teachings about membership in the body (1 Cor. 12:12–31), and warnings about wealth and success (Matt. 19:23–24; Luke 18:23).

We live in a world that does not recognize God as ruler. In many respects, our world is run by money. It is a world in which we take care of ourselves and, to varying degrees, each other. But we do not assume that we can depend on anything other than our own efforts. How can such a worldview possibly result in the formation of a selfless people? By thinking theologically, we embrace the obedience of faith because the Lord "is your life and length of days" (Deut. 30:20 ESV). We can depend on him rather than ourselves. We can trust that our integrity is more important than our bank account.

STEP 3: ACCEPT THE REST THAT GOD PROVIDES.

Finally, we can trust in God's provision to give us rest. When Israel spent forty years in the desert, God gave them all they needed on a day-to-day basis except on the sixth day of the week when he gave them a double portion so that the people could observe a Sabbath on the seventh day. Despite receiving the double portion, some of the people still went out to gather on the seventh day (Exod. 16:24–30).

They did not yet understand the new reality God established when He liberated them from Egypt. The Israelites had only lived under Egyptian rule, which required unceasing labor. They had no sense that God was providing for them in Egypt. If they wanted to eat, they assumed they had to work. But life under God's rule is different. He takes away the pressures we so often feel to sustain ourselves. He offers us a new way of life through his generosity. As God's people, we can then recognize that we have been freed to obey. We can enjoy the restful life Christ promises us because we place hope in God's promise to provide.

Commenting on Matthew 11:28 (NIV), in which Jesus promises rest for those "who are weary and burdened," Moody notes,

> Merchants toil day and night to amass money, in order that they may get rest. Men leave their families and friends and go round the world to earn money, in the hope that they may get rest. Sailors plough the sea and are away from home for months to get money, in order that it may bring them rest. In fact, if rest could be bought in the market, there are many hundreds in London who would be paying a very high price for it; but though money can't buy it,

nevertheless by believing the word of God you can get it without money and without price.[12]

It is no wonder that Moody was entirely free from the love of money. He found his rest in Christ and was more than content with all that God saw fit to provide. Let us do as Moody did. Let us set aside the passing pleasures of the world to find rest and contentment in Christ.

---

12 D. L. Moody, Wondrous Love and Other Gospel Addresses (Frankfort: Outlook, 2020), 86.

WALK IN THE WORD

> "You shall remember that you were a slave in the land of Egypt, and the Lord your God brought you out from there with a mighty hand and an outstretched arm. Therefore the Lord your God commanded you to keep the Sabbath day."
>
> — *Deuteronomy 5:15 ESV*

The exodus from Egypt is one of the most pivotal moments in the Old Testament. By redeeming Israel from slavery, God set in motion a series of events intended to forge Israel into a new sort of nation. Up to that point, all the other nations of the earth were governed by human rulers backed by false gods. Israel would be ruled by the Creator of the universe. Israel would no longer need to depend upon its own efforts to survive and thrive in the world. They would no longer need to follow the logic of Egypt, which demanded that Israel make more bricks with less straw (Exod. 5:5–23). Instead, God commands the Israelites to rest.

The Sabbath command is first given in Exodus 20:8–11 and then reinterpreted in Deuteronomy 5:12–15. The connection between the exodus from Egypt and the Sabbath command is not made explicit in Exodus. Instead, the rationale for Sabbath in Exodus is rooted in the pattern of creation. (Exod. 20:11)

In Deuteronomy, however, as Moses speaks to the people of Israel who are preparing to enter the Promised Land, the connection between the Sabbath and the exodus becomes more crucial. Moses reminds Israel that they are not like the other nations, particularly the nation of Egypt. Rather, they are a nation capable of giving rest to those who labor because God has promised to provide.

In other words, Israel was not delivered from Egypt to recreate Egypt's way of life in the Promised Land. Doing so would prevent Israel from showcasing the power of God. For the world to see the uniqueness of the Lord, Israel had to live according to God's ways. God's ways often ran counter to those of the nations. Israel's prosperity did not depend on the abilities of the Israelite people but on their willingness to obey.

By resting from their work on the seventh day, Israel was affirming that their prosperity was not rooted in the strength and power of the Israelite people but in the power of God. The Sabbath was a reminder that God had not only physically delivered Israel from Egypt but that he had freed the nation to reimagine their way of being in the world. He had freed them for obedience.

We serve the God who freed Israel from Egypt. While we are certainly still supposed to work (2 Thess. 3:10), we should develop a new relationship with money. We no longer serve money or look to it as a source of security. We recognize that money's yoke, unlike that of Christ, is neither easy nor light (Matt. 11:30). When we substitute money for God, we follow a new master that does not allow us to love God with all we are and all we have or to love our neighbor. The logic of money demands that we accumulate more. There is no rest because money demands relentless, unceasing worship and effort to procure it.

Our service to God, however, takes on a much different character. God promises to sustain us so that we are free to obey. Then, as we engage in practices that appear foolish and unproductive to the world, he can showcase his power. We are not loyal to the ways of wealth but to the wisdom of total devotion. It is through our odd, singular devotion to the Lord that we proclaim, "man does not live by bread alone, but man lives by every word that comes from the mouth of the Lord" (Deut. 8:3 ESV).

REFLECTION QUESTIONS

01 | The Bible does not demand poverty, yet it does require that we develop a different sort of relationship with wealth. In what areas of your life have you held on to a relationship with money that looks more like you are living in Egypt and less like you are living in God's kingdom?

02 | What would your life be like if you remembered God's deliverance in the way you handle wealth?

03 | In Colossian 3:5, Paul equates greed with idolatry. How would you explain that association?

04 | What holds us back from embracing God's ways and continuing to depend on money for security and stability?

05 | How might the way we relate to wealth diminish our witness to God? Do you see any specific areas of your economic life that might be detrimental to your ministry?

06 | How might we go about gaining freedom from the love of money?

07 | Having read about this characteristic of Dwight L. Moody, what is your greatest challenge concerning love of money?

08 | What do you envision changing about the way you live your life to relate differently to money?

To move towards becoming more "free from love of money," I will:

07
CONSUMED WITH PASSION FOR THE LOST

> "There is plenty of opportunity in this fallen world to perform works of mercy and religion."
>
> — D. L. Moody,
> *The Ten Commandments*

Dwight Moody was more than an evangelist, yet his evangelistic work and his passion for it cannot be ignored. He preached the gospel in cities across North America and in the United Kingdom. Stanley Gundry, one scholar who studied the life of Dwight Moody, suggests that most estimates about Moody's reach are likely too conservative, even at 100,000,000.[1] According to another Moody scholar named J. Wilbur Chapman, Moody "reached more people during his lifetime than any other man, possibly in the world's history."[2] Moody was the greatest evangelist of his day.

Dwight Moody's desire to see women and men come to Christ drove his evangelistic efforts. That same passion for the lost also served as the foundation for his non-evangelistic ministry activities in educating Christian youth and laypeople as well as engaging in social work among the poor and downtrodden. His work with the poor demonstrated that he "had the genius to develop a programme that worked rather than go down fighting using a model culturally unfit for those he sought to help."[3] Moody believed that everything he did needed to advance the Kingdom of God so that more Christians were prepared to proclaim the gospel to a world that needed to hear it.

As impressive as Moody's formal evangelistic campaigns were, his commitment to sharing the gospel on a more individual level is perhaps the greatest indication of his true passion for souls. Torrey writes, "Mr. Moody made the resolution, shortly after he, himself, was saved, that he would never let twenty-four hours pass over his head without speaking to at least one person about his soul."[4] So Moody did not simply depend on his campaigns to convey the gospel. His passion drove him to engage in a personal, day-to-day ministry as well.

---

1 Stanley Gundry, *Love Them In: The Life and Theology of Dwight Moody* (Grand Rapids: Baker, 1976), 10.
2 J. Wilbur Chapman, *The Life and Work of D. L. Moody* (Philadelphia: American Bible House, 1900), vi.
3 Dorsett, *"D. L. Moody: More than an Evangelist,"* 35.
4 Torrey, *Why God Used D. L. Moody,* 38-39.

Torrey tells the story of a night when Moody realized he had not yet shared the gospel with anyone that day. He spoke to a man who did not respond well to Moody's message. The man then spoke to one of Moody's colleagues, saying that Moody was "doing more harm than he is good." Shaken by what the man had said, Moody began to question whether the man was right. But, as Torrey reports, "Weeks passed by. One night Mr. Moody was in bed when he heard a tremendous pounding at his front door…He opened the door and there stood this man. He said, 'Mr. Moody, I have not had a good night's sleep since that night you spoke to me under the lamppost, and I have come around at this unearthly hour of the night for you to tell me what I have to do to be saved.'"[5] Such were the results of Moody's passion for souls.

MOODY'S PASSION FOR THE POOR

While some scholars have suggested that Moody's passion for souls led him to disconnect the proclamation of the gospel from social action later in his career, Moody saw evangelism and the care for those in need as inseparable.[6] While it was true that Moody tended to focus on individual sin rather than societal concerns, he also knew that the problem of individual sin was not the only problem humanity faced. The problems of society also called for reform.

In 1899 (the year of his death), Moody commented on the challenges associated with big corporations. He recognized the structural challenges and their implications for the poor. He noted, "What can a poor young man do nowadays, unless he goes to work for someone else who is wealthy… trusts, corporations, are bad for young men."[7] His understanding of the

---

5 Torrey, *Why God Used D. L. Moody*, 42.
6 Marsden, *Fundamentalism and American Culture*, 36-37; Paul Louis Metzger, *Consuming Jesus: Beyond Race and Class Divisions in a Consumer Church* (Grand Rapids: Eerdmans, 2007), 19-23.
7 Quoted in Gregg Quiggle, "*An Analysis of Dwight Moody's Urban Social Vision,*" PhD diss., (Open University, 2009), 219.

broader cultural and structural challenges of society likely motivated the foundation of Northfield Seminary and Northfield Mount Hermon School. The schools were founded to provide a Christian education for those who otherwise would receive no education at all.[8] Whatever upward social mobility students might enjoy having completed their education, the primary purpose of the schools was religious: "The motive presented for the pursuit of an education is the power it confers for Christian life and usefulness, not the means it affords to social distinction, or to the gratification of selfish ambition."[9]

Outside of the schools, Moody cared for the poor through a variety of endeavors, even late into his career. Still, he knew he could not serve only the physical needs of the poor. They needed to hear the gospel. Moody saw Matthew 6:33 as requiring that we put God and his righteousness in the highest place even when experiencing hardship. Moody recognized that it was not right to put God in second place even though "a great many people think it is time enough to seek the kingdom of God after they have attended to everything else."[10]

Moody goes on to note, "…it will not do to seek Christ because of what you hope to make by it."[11] He himself admits that he "used to make a mistake on that point."[12] He was referring to the time in his ministry when he would offer the poor food, shelter, and care to open them up to the gospel. However, Moody began to see that by not leading with the gospel, people tended to overlook the great gift of Christ and instead focused on the lesser gifts of the material goods being offered. Moody may have reordered his priorities, but he never stopped caring for the needs of the poor.

---

8 *Hand-Book of the Northfield Seminary and the Mt. Hermon School*, 1889, 13-14.
9 *Hand-Book of the Northfield Seminary and the Mt. Hermon School*, 1889, 12.
10 W. H. Daniels, *Moody: His Words, Work, and Workers* (New York: Nelson and Phillips, 1877), 431.
11 Daniels, *Moody: His Words, Work, and Workers*, 431.
12 Daniels, *Moody: His Words, Work, and Workers*, 431.

Moody did not suggest that caring for the poor was out of line with the gospel. As he notes in his discussion of Nehemiah, "Reading the Bible and remembering the poor—a combination of faith and works—will always bring joy."[13] Rather than advocating for a separation between the gospel and physical aid, Moody simply calls believers to seek God first. It seems clear that "Moody's point was not that Christians should not give to the poor; rather, he was explaining that evangelists and missionaries needed to make sure to keep the gospel at the forefront of their work."[14]

MOODY AND SOCIETAL CONCERNS

Some scholars who look back on Moody's ministry have suggested that he set aside social action to focus solely on evangelism. Despite his evangelistic success, Moody did not disconnect the gospel from what was happening in the world. He did not believe practical acts of Christian kindness and generosity would fix the world any more than he believed that the good news of Jesus Christ could be fully conveyed without good works. As he notes regarding the parable of the Good Samaritan, "Christ has taught us very clearly that any man or woman who is in need of our love and our help—whether temporal or spiritual—is our neighbour. If we can render them any service we are to do it in the name of our Master."[15] He goes on to suggest,

> This Samaritan did not pull a manuscript out of his pocket, and begin to read a long sermon to the wounded man. Some people seem to think that all the world needs is a lot of sermons. Why, the people of this land have been almost preached to death. What we want is to preach more sermons with our hands and feet—to carry the Gospel to people by acts of kindness.[16]

---

13 D. L. Moody, *Men of the Bible* (Chicago: The Bible Institute Colportage Association, 1898, 67.
14 Greg Quiggle, "An Analysis of Dwight Moody's Urban Social Vision," 262.
15 Moody, *To the Work! To the Work!*, 91.
16 Moody, *To the Work! To the Work!*, 94.

Moody's evangelistic ministry demanded that the gospel be preached. The gospel "is the power of God for salvation to everyone who believes" (Rom. 1:16 ESV). To set the preaching of the gospel aside to focus on social and political concerns could only make the world more comfortable, not less broken. As Moody puts it, "Whitewashing the pump won't make the water pure."[17] In other words, any change that did not involve Christ would be superficial. Human efforts to make the world a better place can never overcome sin and death. Christ must be preached.

Moody believed in the power of personal conversion. As William Moody writes, "He [Dwight Moody] insisted that the most efficacious means of reformation was through the individual."[18] He felt it was essential because it is through one's acceptance of Christ that the Holy Spirit enters our life. If, as Moody believed, we are all ruined by sin, there was little hope that changing the world without redeeming the soul would keep sin at bay. Whatever we had fixed would soon be broken again. However, he believed that individuals enlivened by the Holy Spirit and committed to following Christ, seeking restitution for past wrongs, giving generously to assist the poor, and avoiding trappings that contribute to societal ills would point the way to the Kingdom of God.

Moody never stopped believing that individual sin was at the root of all humanity's problems, especially the way human sin impacted the poor. His various critiques of callous employment practices and wealth were an expression of his Christ-centered view of the world. He said,

> We have too much wealth and too much poverty. Why don't some of the people who have made their fortunes stop and go out into the highways and byways and help the poor? That's my idea of socialism, and it's founded on the ideas of Christ.[19]

---

17 Quoted in Myron Chartier, *The Social Views of Dwight. L. Moody and Their Relation to the Workman of 1860-1900* (Fort Hayes: Fort Hays Kansas State College, 1969), 31.
18 Moody, *The Life of Dwight L. Moody*, 170.
19 Quoted in Quiggle, "An Analysis of Dwight Moody's Urban Social Vision," 218.

Moody didn't just criticize. He helped. During the Civil War, for instance, Moody helped establish an employment bureau to assist wounded soldiers after the war.[20] Following the Chicago fire, Moody had a temporary shelter built and raised funds to provide food and spiritual support for those who had lost their homes.[21]

THE CALL OF DISCIPLESHIP

For Moody, proclaiming the gospel was a holistic activity. His passion for souls was inseparable from his love for people and his desire to build the church. Moody believed mass conversions were necessary. He also believed the church sorely needed disciples deeply committed to the cause of Christ. Lyle Dorsett, who wrote a biography on Dwight Moody, comments,

> Moody took the view that Christ's great commission calls us to make disciples, not mere converts (Matt. 28.18–20). Consequently, he laboured incessantly to help people grow up into strong, reproducing disciples, and he strove to equip people to become full-time workers in this broader disciple-making work of rescuing, healing and nurturing souls.[22]

In this sense, Moody's passion for souls was also a passion not simply to grow the church numerically but to build the body of Christ so that "through the church the manifold wisdom of God might now be made known" (Eph. 3:10 ESV).

Moody did not see his ministry as narrowly evangelistic. He realized early on in his ministry as a Civil War chaplain the difference between those who "were ready to meet the One they loved and served" and those "who

---

20 J. Wilbur Chapman, *The Life and Work of Dwight L. Moody* (Philadelphia: American Bible House, 1900), 151.
21 W. H. Daniels, *Moody: His Words, Work, and Workers* (New York: Nelson and Phillips, 1877), 37.
22 Lyle W. Dorsett, *"D. L. Moody: More than an Evangelist,"* in Mr. Moody and the Evangelical Tradition ed. Timothy George (New York: Continuum, 2004), 31-32.

had never experienced healing, revealed no true relationship with Christ or had only a passing acquaintance with him."[23] He "grew convinced that the differences he observed could be attributed to one thing—care for the soul."[24] Having seen the stark contrast between a well-fed Christian and a malnourished Christian, Moody dedicated himself to ensuring that those who came to Christ through his evangelistic efforts were positioned to grow in the faith thereafter. As such,

> Moody took what he learned in the tent hospitals and applied it throughout his ministry…From the lay training programmes to the inquiry rooms, he led the people from listening and prayer to carefully making certain that each soul had a church with a pastor or lay leader who would purposively follow up…[25]

He desired to see the church activated and empowered to serve the Lord. His concern was not to fill pews with converts but to add power to the church. As he says,

> Sometimes you can take one hundred members into the Church, and they don't add to its power. Now that is all wrong. If they were only anointed by the Spirit of God, there would be great power if one hundred saved ones were added to the Church.[26]

Evangelistic campaigns alone could not accomplish Moody's goal of making disciples. As such, he shifted away from certain practices, including the use of the "anxious bench" used by other evangelists of his day to the inquiry room "where those whose spiritual concern had been heightened by the service could come for further information and counsel in a quiet setting."[27]

---

23 Dorsett, *"D. L. Moody: More than an Evangelist,"* 34.
24 Dorsett, *"D. L. Moody: More than an Evangelist,"* 34.
25 Dorsett, *"D. L. Moody: More than an Evangelist,"* 34.
26 Moody, *Secret Power,* 47.
27 Stanley N. Gundry, *"Demythologizing Moody,"* in Mr. Moody and the Evangelical Tradition ed. Timothy George (New York: Continuum, 2004), 19-20.

His educational endeavors were, in part, a solution to the lack of trained Christian workers to assist in his revivals. Moody saw the education of God's people as essential for enhancing his evangelistic efforts because once an individual accepted Christ, they would ultimately need someone to walk with them as they embraced the Christian life. Training individuals to be capable of making disciples was an extension of Moody's passion for the lost.

SHOWCASING PASSION FOR THE LOST

As we seek to proclaim the gospel in our day, what can we learn from Moody to help us demonstrate our passion for the lost?

STEP 1: PREACH THE GOSPEL.

We cannot expect people to respond to the gospel message if they never hear it. We have to preach the gospel. Moody understood that sharing the gospel message was of utmost importance, and it was something that everyone needed to hear. As he observed,

> There is no class of people exempt from broken hearts. The rich and the poor suffer alike…I have found there are as many broken hearts among the learned as the unlearned, the cultured as the uncultured, the rich as the poor.[28]

The gospel message applies to every neighbor regardless of her or his position in this world. If we truly love our neighbors, we will tell them about the gift of salvation offered to all who believe in Jesus Christ.

STEP 2: GROW IN FAITH.

Second, Moody understood that the work of the gospel does not stop at conversion. He made efforts to nurture the souls of those who made a profession of faith, seeking to fill the body of Christ with power. Today, we need to adopt a similar spirit. We must develop our own faith and the faith of others by deepening our commitment to Christ and increasing our reliance on the Holy Spirit.

---

28 D. L. Moody, *New Sermons, Addresses, and Prayers* (New York: Henry S. Goodspeed & Co., 1877), 211.

STEP 3: LOVE YOUR NEIGHBOR.

Finally, we cannot neglect the physical needs of others. We face a myriad of challenges today. Christians cannot turn a blind eye to those who need assistance or are marginalized in society. Instead, we are to demonstrate our love for God in concrete acts of love for others. We are to be good neighbors to all who are in need within our fallen world.

Moody's passion for the lost was impressive. Though it is often represented as a more straightforward zeal for personal and mass evangelism, his passion drove him to care for and disciple new converts and to assist those in need. In many ways, Moody's passion for the lost was the most significant factor influencing his life and ministry. He knew that saving souls would have an everlasting impact because "if you turn one to Christ, that one may turn a hundred; they may turn a thousand, and so the stream, small at first, goes on broadening and deepening as it rolls toward eternity."[29]

---

29 Moody, *To the Work! To the Work!*, 144.

WALK IN THE WORD

"If anyone thinks he is religious and does not bridle his tongue but deceives his heart, this person's religion is worthless. Religion that is pure and undefiled before God the Father is this: to visit orphans and widows in their affliction, and to keep oneself unstained from the world."

— James 1:26-27 ESV

When Jesus is asked which commandment is the greatest, he answers,
> You shall love the Lord your God with all your heart and with all your soul and with all your mind. This is the great and first commandment. And a second is like it: You shall love your neighbor as yourself. On these two commandments depend all the law and the prophets (Matt. 22:37–40 ESV).

Jesus ties together our love for God and neighbor. His answer points to the all-encompassing nature of the Christian life. We cannot divorce the spiritual from the physical. Sharing the gospel without demonstrating our belief in concrete ways leaves our witness of Christ incomplete. We can't engage in humanitarian efforts without proclaiming the gospel to women and men who do not know Christ. The two great commandments belong together and cannot be separated. The love of God is expressed as a love for one's neighbors. The love of one's neighbors reflects our allegiance to God.

As James discusses these matters, he does not speak in terms of love but of faith. He notes,
> What good is it, my brothers, if someone says he has faith but does not have works? Can that faith save him? If a brother or sister is poorly clothed and lacking in daily food, and one of you says to them, "Go in peace, be warmed and filled," without giving them the things needed for the body, what good is that? So also faith by itself, if it does not have works is dead (James 2:14–17 ESV).

The point is that a faith that does not produce works is not really faith. If our faith in God does not change the way we live, we must ask ourselves whether we have faith at all.

Ultimately, God does not want us to wear a cross or get our favorite Bible verse tattooed across our wrist. Such professions can certainly be powerful, but they cannot be powerful alone. They must be accompanied by the activities that showcase commitment to "religion that is pure and undefiled before God the Father," which means caring for the downtrodden of society (James 1:27 ESV).

There are surely times when, like Peter, we may need to say that we have no silver or gold but can give Christ and his blessings instead (Acts 3:6). Yet, we must never hide behind the gospel if we have an opportunity to proclaim Christ by meeting the needs of those around us. To have a passion for the lost, we must also have a passion for God. We must love God and love our neighbors. As we give all we are and all we have to the Lord, he will ultimately direct us to those he desires us to help. And if we do so, we fulfill the two greatest commandments at once and give glory to God as well!

REFLECTION QUESTIONS

01 | How would you describe the connection between the first and second greatest commandments in your own words?

02 | In what ways have you separated the first and second greatest commandments in your own life?

03 | How have you shown your love for neighbors lately?

04 | Who are some of the people around you who might benefit from your care?

05 | Try to describe how you can love God without loving others.

06 | How might we go about cultivating a passion for the lost?

07 | Having explored this characteristic of D.L. Moody, do you think you have passion for the lost? Why or why not?

08 | What do you think you need to change to have more passion for the lost?

To move towards becoming more "passionate for the lost," I will:

08
IMBUED WITH POWER FROM ON HIGH

> "Some people seem to think they are losing time if they wait on God for His power, and so away they go and work without unction; they are working without any anointing, they are working without any power."
>
> – D. L. Moody,
> *Secret Power*

R. A. Torrey tells the story of two Methodist women who had a profound influence on Dwight Moody. In 1871, Auntie Cook and Mrs. Snow told Moody they were praying for him. Moody didn't understand why they would pray for him instead of praying for the lost. They explained that they were praying for Moody to be baptized by the Holy Spirit. Moody prayed with the women and continued to pray on his own until, in Torrey's words,

> Not long after, one day on his way to England, he was walking up Wall Street in New York (Mr. Moody very seldom told this and I almost hesitate to tell it) and in the midst of the bustle and hurry of that city his prayer was answered; the power of God fell upon him as he walked up the street and he had to hurry off to the house of a friend and ask that he might have a room by himself, and in that room he stayed alone for hours; and the Holy Ghost came upon him filling his soul with such joy that at last he had to ask God to withhold His hand, lest he die on the spot from very joy.[1]

Beyond Moody's joy, the power of the Holy Spirit carried Moody to London where "the power of God wrought through him mightily in North London and hundreds were added to the churches, and that was what led to his being invited over to the wonderful campaign that followed in later years."[2]

This rather early experience with the Holy Spirit stayed with Moody. While he believed that all those who had accepted Jesus Christ as their Lord and Savior had received the Holy Spirit, he also believed that there was a difference between "the work of the Holy Spirit on and in the believer."[3] Dependence on the Spirit became a cornerstone of Moody's theology and ministry. As he notes, "The Gospel proclamation cannot be

---
1 Torrey, *Why God Used D. L. Moody*, 53.
2 Torrey, *Why God Used D. L. Moody*, 53-54.
3 Quiggle, *"An Analysis of Dwight Moody's Urban Social Vision,"* 194.

divorced from the Holy Spirit. Unless He attend the word in power, vain will be the attempt in preaching it."[4]

THE CHURCH IN NUMBER AND POWER

Moody's understanding of the Holy Spirit was forged through his experiences in ministry during the 1800s. Moody believed deeply in the need for believers to be enlivened by a special work of the Holy Spirit. He saw it as crucial to the life of the church. While we may think that Moody was primarily interested in church growth because of his emphasis on evangelism, Moody had no interest in growing the church's number without increasing its power.

Speaking of the sort of power the church needs, Moody explains,

> Doctor Gordon of Boston used to say that as you passed along Washington Street of that city, or Broadway, New York, you might see stores with the card in the window, 'To rent, with or without power,' and anyone could rent the store, and by paying something extra could have power furnished from the engine in the rear. Doctor Gordon thought it would be a good thing to ask men and women when they joined the church if they wanted to be a member on the 'with power' or the 'without power' basis, and if the latter, to tell them there were no vacancies for that kind in the church, it already had too many members without power.[5]

Moody would not have wanted to keep individuals from the church, but he was not aiming simply to add to the church's numbers. He desired to see the church empowered by the Spirit. As he asserts,

> This is the Church's need today; we want the Spirit to come in mighty power and consume all the vile dross there is in us. Oh! that

---
4 Moody, *Secret Power*, 13.
5 D. L. Moody, *Moody's Latest Sermons* (Chicago: The Bible Institute Colportage Association, 1900), 20.

> the Spirit of fire may come down and burn everything in us that is contrary to God's blessed Word and Will.[6]

Moody believed that the church was too dependent on tactics that kept it at an arm's distance from God. He feared that the church was too often "like an army being defeated because it refuses to use its weapons."[7] He recognized that the church needed more workers who had the power of the Spirit. He had a keen understanding of what the church was lacking. Though "a great many people are thinking we need new measures, that we need new churches, that we need new organs, and that we need new choirs, and all these new things," Dwight Moody saw matters differently.[8] He believed what was needed was "the old power that the Apostles had; that is what we want, and if we have that in our churches, there will be new life."[9] So, rather than seeking "men who were possessed of natural gifts, of eloquence, and of pulpit power, but didn't have Holy Ghost power," the church needed to be looking for those who had opened themselves up to being conduits for the Holy Spirit.[10]

BAPTISM IN THE SPIRIT

It was obvious to all his contemporaries that Moody was open to the Holy Spirit. His desire to see the church empowered by the Spirit led him to call on others to preach on the topic. Torrey recalls, "Time and again, when a call came to me to off to some church, he would come up to me and say: 'Now, Torrey, be sure and preach on the baptism of the Holy Ghost.' I do not know how many times he said that to me."[11]

---

6 Moody, *Secret Power*, 69.
7 Dorsett, *A Passion for Souls*, 348.
8 Moody, *Secret Power*, 35.
9 Moody, *Secret Power*, 35.
10 Moody, *New Sermons, Addresses, and Prayers*, 681.
11 Torrey, *Why God Used D. L. Moody*, 55.

Beyond a desire to have the baptism of the Holy Spirit preached, Moody himself sought the Spirit's power. William Moody writes, "For a year or more before he left Chicago he was continually burdened and crying to God for more power. Then he was always wanting to get a few people together for half a day of prayer and would groan and weep before God for the baptism of the Spirit."[12] Moody's groaning and weeping did not necessarily mean he felt anxious or inadequate to serve in ministry. Instead, Moody was anxious to avoid building a following in his own power because he felt inadequate to do the work of God without the Holy Spirit. His groaning and weeping were not a sign of weakness but of his utter desire to follow God. He wanted to be led by the Spirit.

As much as Moody yearned for the Spirit's power, he also saw a need to avoid quenching or grieving the Holy Spirit. He recognized that God's people could resist the Spirit's power. Whether it was "theatrical performances, and fairs, and fashions," disunity among God's people, or the resistance of individual Christians, Moody saw that there were plenty of ways God's people can quench or grieve the Spirit.[13] And to grieve the Spirit was to rob the church of power. To walk in our own power is to misrepresent God. We can claim to be following the Spirit's leading while living as if he does not exist. It is up to us to constantly question,

> how it is that we have, in the midst of our agendas, strategies, moral outrage, and legitimate concerns, fashioned God into a deity of our own making so that He looks increasingly like us rather than us being transformed to look increasingly like Him?[14]

When we think about the Holy Spirit today, there is much we can learn from Moody. For him, the Holy Spirit was essential for the church. The Holy Spirit's presence in the lives of God's people was never in question, but Moody was concerned that God's people would relegate the Holy

---

12 Moody, *The Life of D. L. Moody*, 261.
13 Moody, *New Sermons, Addresses, and Prayers*, 681.
14 Spencer, *Thinking Christian*, 176.

Spirit to the margins of their day-to-day lives. We must leave the space necessary "to have the sort of slow, deliberate dialogues that reflect our deep conviction that discerning the Spirit is crucial to offering faithful testimony."[15] In other words, we must be intentional about our desire for the Spirit to move within our lives. We must be patient and watch for the Holy Spirit's leading.

BAPTISM IN SPIRIT IN THE WORD

In his 1994 book about the Holy Spirit in the letters of Paul, New Testament scholar Gordon Fee suggested that the Holy Spirit has been "largely marginalized in our actual life together as a community of faith."[16] Looking back on Fee's assertion almost three decades later, it's hard to deny that many within the community of faith continue to marginalize the Holy Spirit. We must recapture a sense of true dependence upon the Spirit's power and set aside even those good things in our lives that are quenching the Holy Spirit. As Moody says,

> If I love my family more than God, then I am quenching the Spirit of God within me; if I love wealth, if I love fame, if I love honor, if I love position, if I love pleasure, if I love self, more than I love God who created and saved me, then I am committing a sin; I am not only grieving the Spirit of God, but quenching Him, and robbing my soul of His power.[17]

Clearly, we can accomplish much on our own without the Spirit because of what God has given us. In Genesis 11:1–9, we see all the people of the earth coming together. They use their God-given gifts to build a city and a tower so that they can avoid being scattered across the face of the earth. Because they speak the same language (Gen 11:1) and have the appropriate technologies (Gen 11:3–4), they believe they have the

---
15 Spencer, *Thinking Christian*, 174.
16 Gordon D. Fee, *God's Empowering Presence: The Holy Spirit in the Letters of Paul* (Peabody: Hendrickson, 1994), 1.
17 Moody, *Secret Power*, 114.

capacity to make a name for themselves and take it. While it is tempting to look at the people's plans and assume they will fail, God offers a different assessment: "If as one people speaking the same language they have begun to do this, then nothing they plan to do will be impossible for them" (Gen. 11:6 NIV). God affirms their ability to do what they have set out to do and determines to intervene.

Whether measured in the form of a completed city and tower, the size of one's church, or the amount of money a ministry raises, success is not necessarily a sign that we are following the Spirit of God and walking in his power. If we gauge the degree to which God is involved in a ministry based on that ministry's size or on achieving some lofty goal, we simplify the complex relationship between process and outcomes. We tend to assume that when something turns out well, the strategy and process were obviously good. Yet, "a failed outcome…does not necessarily mean the decision or decision process behind it was bad. There are good decisions with bad outcomes…Evaluating decisions and outcomes separately is equally important in the opposite case: bad decisions may occasionally result in good outcomes."[18] Still, we continue to assume that if an individual or ministry affirms the right doctrinal positions, preaches the word faithfully, and sees growth in their ministry, the Spirit of the Lord is obviously at work.

Moody would disagree. He had a large ministry by anyone's measure. Despite his lack of formal education, he was a talented individual whose earnestness, ambition, and willingness to learn were impressive. But the genius of Moody's ministry is not found in some strategy, tactic, or talent. He wasn't successful because of his natural charisma, outstanding speaking voice, or eloquent prose. He was successful because he relentlessly sought God's empowering presence and recognized that doing ministry without the power of the Holy Spirit was an act of futility.

18 Safi Bahcall, *Loonshots: How to Nurture the Crazy Ideas that Win Wars, Cure Diseases, and Transform Industries* (New York: St. Martin's, 2019), 142.

BECOMING EMPOWERED

Moody's life and ministry offer several lessons which can benefit the church today. We cannot be empowered without obeying God's word and opening ourselves up for the Holy Spirit to work in our lives.

STEP 1: BE AWARE OF THE SPIRIT.

Moody spent a great deal of time thinking and speaking about the Holy Spirit. We don't. As such, it is difficult to believe that we are well-positioned to experience the sort of power Moody experienced. If we don't embrace the Spirit's work in our lives, it seems unlikely that we will avoid serving God in our own power. If we are to be empowered by the Spirit, we must develop a theology of the Spirit that alerts us to his ongoing work in our lives and the power he makes available to us as we yield to God's will.

STEP 2: TRUST THE SPIRIT.

There is nothing extraordinary about Dwight Moody that should have allowed him to do all that he did. Ambitious as he was, Dwight and Emma Moody were exhausted by the time they made their first trip to the United Kingdom in 1867 after only about five years of ministry. Had Moody continued to minister in his own power, God would never have been able to accomplish all he did through Moody. The church in our age will never have the capacity to accomplish all God desires. No matter how gifted we are, we are limited beings. We need God's power. We cannot become enamored with the results we achieve on our own because they may well pale in comparison to all that God could do if we allowed the Holy Spirit to work through us.

STEP 3: DEPEND ON THE SPIRIT.

Finally, whatever one may think of his formal discussions of theology, Moody was a man who was deeply committed to living in the world in light of God's presence and truth. Moody committed himself to consistently waiting on God. While we would be going too far to suggest that Moody was always in step with the Spirit, Moody fervently sought to be empowered by him. He did not depend on tactics (though he did use them) but desired to be a vehicle for the Spirit's power. It was that desire that fueled Moody's ministry. Moody accomplished more in his sixty-two years than most would in twice that time. However, the volume of Moody's work was not the secret to his success. It was his utter dependence on the Spirit that gave him his power.

The church in any age would do well to remember that God's work is not dependent on slick presentations or entertaining worship. It is accomplished by his power working in and through his people. We must seek the power of the Holy Spirit. Let us be a people willing to wait for God's power so that we may accomplish his will rather than doing our own.

WALK IN THE WORD

"Some of you have become arrogant, as if I were not coming to you. But I will come to you very soon, if the Lord is willing, and then I will find out not only how these arrogant people are talking, but what power they have. For the Kingdom of God is not a matter of talk but of power."

– 1 Corinthians 4:18–20 NIV

God gives people platforms. He places them in positions of influence and responsibility. Yet, whatever prominence God provides, some want to elevate themselves even higher. We tend to allow those with big ministries and big influence to overshadow God. We forget God and focus instead on a given individual's skill, savvy, and charisma. If we depend upon the capabilities of those who lead us, it not only diminishes God but also puts those leaders in the awkward position of living up to unrealistic expectations. When we ask those who lead us to carry loads only God can lift, we can be sure we have made them into idols "fashioned by human hands" (2 Kings 19:18; 2 Chron. 32:19; Ps. 115:4; 135:15; Isa. 37:19; Acts 19:26).

When Paul writes to the church in Corinth, he is addressing something akin to a cult of personality. The Corinthians have set aside their unity in Christ to pledge their allegiance to a particular leader, thus creating division in the body. As Paul writes,

> …each one of you says, "I follow Paul," or "I follow Apollos," or "I follow Cephas," or "I follow Christ." Is Christ divided? Was Paul crucified for you? Or were you baptized in the name of Paul? I thank God that I baptized none of you except Crispus and Gaius, so that no one may say that you were baptized in my name…For Christ did not send me to baptize but to preach the gospel, and not with words of eloquent wisdom, lest the cross of Christ be emptied of its power (1 Cor. 1:12–17 ESV).

Divided in this way, the church denies Christ his central place. They empty the cross of Christ of its power because they do not lean on it. Instead, they depend on convincing rhetoric, persuasive speech, and the sheer force of their presence to win people over to their faction. Even if they preach Jesus, they have lost because they have diminished the gospel by substituting the unlimited power of the Spirit with our meager human resources.

Paul reminds the Corinthians that his own speech and message were "not in plausible words of wisdom, but in demonstration of the Spirit and of power, so that your faith might not rest in the wisdom of men but in the power of God" (1 Cor. 2:4–5 ESV). Those who deliver the gospel do not seek to draw people to themselves or to attract people with their own personal magnetism. Instead, they point others away from themselves and toward Jesus Christ.

We must take care not to lose sight of Christ by becoming too enamored with those who preach the gospel. We must also take care not to draw people to ourselves rather than leading them to Christ. As we learn to trust in the Spirit's power, we will also learn to exercise restraint in the use of our gifts. We learn to allow God to work through our weakness because "God chose what is foolish in the world to shame the wise; God chose what is weak in the world to shame the strong" (1 Cor. 1:27 ESV).

REFLECTION QUESTIONS

01 | What does Paul mean when he says that "the Kingdom of God is not a matter of talk but of power" (1 Cor 4:20)?

02 | To what extent are you "following Apollos" rather than following Christ and affirming the unity of the church?

03 | Where do you see the modern-day church leaning too heavily on charisma or rhetoric as opposed to God's power?

04 | How would you reconcile Paul's teaching about the unity of Christ's body in a day and age when many Christian speakers and pastors have national and international platforms and develop something of a following? How can we combat the same challenges that arose in Corinth given the rise of the Christian influencer today?

05 | What might it look like for you to restrain the use of your gifts? How can you operate from a position of weakness?

06 | How might we go about experiencing the power of the Holy Spirit as Moody did?

07 | Having read about this characteristic of Dwight L. Moody, how "imbued with power" do you think you are?

08 | What do you think you need to change about the way you live to become more empowered with the Spirit?

To move towards becoming more "empowered," I will:

09

UNDISTRACTED

> "It doesn't take long to build the walls of a city if you can only get the whole of the people at it. If the Christians of this country would only rise up, we could evangelize America in twelve months."
>
> – D. L. Moody,
> *Men of the Bible*

There are many calls for social reform in the Old Testament prophetic books. Hosea critiques the use of dishonest scales to cheat people in the marketplace (Hos. 12:7). Jeremiah warns the people of Judah not to be fooled by the presence of God's temple but to change the way they treat the foreigners, fatherless, and widows (Jer. 7:4–7). Isaiah proclaims God's opposition to those who make unjust laws that would "deprive the poor of their rights and withhold justice from the oppressed of my people, making widows their prey and robbing the fatherless" (Isa. 10:1–2 NIV). God takes notice of the systems and structures that disregard the way he has ordered the world. He does not take lightly the authorities that deny dignity to those made in his image.

The prophetic critiques of injustice and abuse of power are not as concerned with social reform as they might initially appear. The prophets are not concerned with justice as an abstract idea. For the prophets, Israel's practice of justice was a sign of their ongoing commitment to the Lord. Justice was a means for the nation to demonstrate its trust in the Lord. A people who truly embraced the ways of God had no need to cheat, promote falsehoods, or oppress the poor and the needy. Surely God also appoints rulers and authorities to maintain order and to enact justice in some sense, yet for God's people, to act justly reflects their conviction to live according to God's order even when doing so is inconvenient.

Christians are certainly right to pursue justice and to speak truth to those in power. Working toward social reform, however, should not overshadow the theological proclamation and work that only those who know Christ can do. Social reform cannot be separated from the broader mission of the church to "Go therefore and make disciples of all nations, baptizing them in the name of the Father and the Son and of the Holy

Spirit, teaching them to observe all that I have commanded you" (Matt. 28:19–20 ESV).

Dwight Moody's concern was that Christians would not be distracted from the Great Commission as they sought to address the evils of the world. Clearly, Moody believed in assisting those in need. Yet Moody saw assisting those in need as wrapped up with the gospel. In Moody's mind, fixing the world was not possible without the salvation of souls because there was no other way to defeat sin. As such, he was critical of strategies that allowed political solutions to overshadow the gospel:

> I have seen many Christian men on the plain of Ono, men who were doing a splendid work but had been switched off. Think how much work has been neglected by temperance advocates in this country because they have gone into politics and into discussing woman's rights and woman's suffrage. How many times the Young Men's Christian Association has been switched off by discussing some other subject instead of holding up Christ before a lost world! If the church would only keep right on and build the walls of Jerusalem, they would soon be built. Oh, it is a wily devil that we have to contend with! Do you know it? If he can only get the church to stop to discuss these questions, he has accomplished his desire.[1]

Moody was aware that the systems of the world needed to be addressed. Yet, he did not want God's people to become so consumed with solving the world's problems through secular or governmental means that they neglected the cause of Christ. Moody knew that "there are some now who think they can legislate men back to God—that they can prevent sin by legislation," but he always believed the final solution to sin and

---
1 Moody, *Men of the Bible*, 65.

death is found through faith in Jesus Christ. He therefore sought to be undistracted by man's solutions, believing they had no ultimate effect.[2]

A narrow reading of D. L. Moody's work could lead one to assume he was simply against Christian participation in government or politics. In reality, he wanted Christians to engage in activities that would bring about lasting, eternal changes. He was not opposed to Christians participating in politics. Instead, he was opposed to Christians leaving the gospel on the sidelines in order to pursue economic or political solutions to the challenges facing the world: "In all departments of life you find that men are very anxious for a revival in the things that concern them most. If this is legitimate—and I do not say but it is perfectly right in its place—should not every child of God be praying for and desiring a revival of godliness in the world at the present time?"[3] Again, we see that Moody is less concerned with Christians engaging in business or politics than he is about ensuring that Christians do what they alone can do: proclaim the gospel to the world and call upon the Lord to bring revival.

MOODY'S CONTROVERSY

We may seek to live for Christ in an undistracted manner. We may even faithfully follow the Holy Spirit. No matter how faithful we are, we still live in a fallen world. As such, our actions will most likely have negative consequences. The world is like a baby's mobile. Touching one side makes all the other sides move. Because our decisions are seldom made in isolation, we can't always predict how our given decision will influence the world around us. Put differently, making decisions within a fallen world is often a wonderful way to showcase our limitations. There are moments when we must choose to follow some of our convictions even when doing so requires us to compromise others. Dwight Moody faced

---

2 Dwight L. Moody, *To the Work! To the Work!: Exhortations to Christians* (Toronto: Rose, 1885), 93.
3 Dwight L. Moody, *To the Work! To the Work!*, 10.

such a choice as he sought to continue his evangelistic work in the post-Civil War South.

Racial tensions continued to plague the United States after the Civil War ended. African Americans were free, but they were still facing widespread prejudices woven into the socio-political fabric of the country. More troubling, many whites continued to view African Americans as something less than fully human. These broader societal challenges were matched by challenges in the Christian community related to "two great problems in practical theology."[4] The first problem "was the prominence of racism, which continued with mob rule and the rope just as it had with the chain and the lash."[5] The second problem "was the expansion of consumer capitalism, in which the temptations to create easy wealth were matched by large-scale alienation and considerable poverty in both urban and rural America."[6]

The problem of racism touched Moody's ministry directly. In 1876, Moody planned an evangelistic campaign in Augusta, Georgia. Local white leaders pressed Moody to segregate the meeting. Despite his initial opposition to the request, Moody ultimately agreed to segregate the meeting. He continued to do so into the mid-1890s.

His actions seem to demonstrate his conviction that individual conversion was needed before anything could change in society. Yet his decision, as rooted as it may have been in his theological convictions regarding the gospel, also stood in tension with his convictions regarding the unity of the body of Christ. To many, Moody's decision to hold segregated campaigns was a tacit authorization of ongoing prejudice against African Americans. Even though Moody desired to see unity in the church, his decision to hold segregated meetings made him a divisive figure.

---

[4] Mark A. Noll, *The Civil War as a Theological Crisis* (Chapel Hill: The University of North Carolina Press, 2006), 159.
[5] Noll, *The Civil War as a Theological Crisis*, 159.
[6] Noll, *The Civil War as a Theological Crisis*, 159.

In Atlanta, by conceding to the demands of local whites, Moody did so in conflict with his own beliefs concerning the segregation of races in religious meetings. Moody did not acquiesce to the Southern pastors without making clear his views on the issue of segregation. One reporter notes,

> When he [Moody] first began holding his open-air meetings here, negroes mingled so indiscriminately with the audience that it became disagreeable to the whites, and a dividing fence was put up. Mr. Moody did not like this, and spoke of it, when one of our Pastors informed him that it was impossible for blacks and whites to mingle even in a religious audience. Mr. Moody then said, "I see you have not gotten over your rebellious feelings yet."[7]

As a result of sharing his views on segregation, Moody lost the approval of some Southern whites. As the reporter notes concerning the incident in Atlanta, "I was disposed to like Mr. Moody, and heard him with pleasure until this circumstance occurred. But now I feel differently toward him, and I furthermore will venture to say that as soon as it is generally known, the loyal gentleman will have very few to hear him among the whites."[8]

Whatever credibility Moody lost among Southern whites, his segregated campaigns drew more vocal criticism from the African American church. His meeting in Charleston, South Carolina, was denounced at the New York Annual Conference of the African Church of 1887. A New York Times piece reports Dr. Tanner, a pastor at the conference, saying, "Our report should condemn Dwight L. Moody. His conduct toward the negroes during his Southern tour has been shameless."[9] Moody's decision was creating controversy and casting shade on Moody's efforts to proclaim the gospel.

---

7 New York Times. 11 Dec 1876.
8 New York Times. 11 Dec 1876.
9 New York Times. 11 June 1887.

CONFLICTING CONVICTIONS

Moody's segregated meetings were not rooted in racism. While we don't know exactly why he chose to continue holding the segregated meetings, Moody's other decisions and perspectives throughout his ministry may offer some hints as to his rationale. Less controversial than the segregated meetings, Moody's choice to distance himself from the temperance movement and his critique of Mission Churches suggest that Moody was caught between two convictions in his decision to hold segregated meetings.

One such choice was related to a partnership with the temperance movement. When he separated from Frances E. Willard, who was the head of the Women's Christian Temperance Union, he did so because of her overemphasis on abstinence from alcohol, which he believed was overshadowing the gospel and creating unnecessary tensions within the body of Christ. Moody biographer Dorsett notes, "The wedge was a two-edged sword that Willard carried with her into evangelistic work—temperance and feminism. She insisted on pushing temperance (actually total abstinence from alcohol) in almost every gathering where she presided."[10] While Moody largely agreed with Willard about the potential dangers of alcohol, he was well aware that "many mainline clergy and laity did social drinking, and Moody was more interested in unity than the cause of prohibition."[11] Not wanting to alienate anyone from hearing the Bible preached, Moody chose not to maintain a close affiliation with the Women's Christian Temperance Union. Instead, he opted to preach the gospel rather than pressing into this particular social issue.

---

10 Dorsett, *Passion for Souls*, 253.
11 Dorsett, *Passion for Souls*, 253.

Moody's decision to part ways with Frances Willard illustrates his decision-making process for segregating his evangelistic meetings in the South. Willard's message had the potential to divide God's people and keep them from hearing the gospel, and Moody did not believe the problems of society could be solved apart from the gospel. To preach abstinence rather than Christ would create an unnecessary divide and stumbling block for some within the church. Moody believed that when women and men accepted Christ, the Holy Spirit would convict them and lead them to repentance. To deprive the church of God's word and unbelievers of the gospel would leave women and men with little opportunity to change.

Moody also critiqued mission churches. He was convinced that these churches were reinforcing class distinctions rather than drawing the church together. Many thought he believed that the wealthy needed to convert the poor. Speaking at a horse show, Moody notes,

> I don't believe in mission churches. I don't indorse [sic] the work of Fifth Avenue people for the conversion of the east side…If there are any of you here who attended the Horse Show lately, I say to you, if you want to show off and exercise your fat horses you can do it by giving drives to the poor in Central Park.[12]

Moody believed that giving money to the poor without showing them love, care, and respect was out of line with the gospel. He goes on to suggest, "Dr. John Hall, Dr. Van Dyke, and Dr. Parkhurst are all great preachers, but if the women of Fifth Avenue will but drive poor invalids around the Park, they will preach a more eloquent sermon than any of these eminent gentlemen can deliver."[13]

Moody's opposition to the mission churches was also rooted in deeply held convictions. Christians should be unified, not separated. In the

---

12 New York Times. 18 Nov 1896.
13 New York Times. 18 Nov 1896.

mission churches, Moody saw a structuring of relationships that was detrimental to the poor. Many disagreed with him. As one of Moody's opponents suggests, "His [Moody's] condemnation of purely mission churches as tending to promote and perpetuate class distinctions, and of the grinding of the faces of the poor by the rich, is hardly qualified."[14] As Moody saw it, when the rich used their money to remain at arm's length from the poor, they were not showing love for their neighbor. God's people should not be artificially divided because some within the body had been gifted with wealth. The body of Christ is to be a united community in part because "The Spirit of God don't work where there is division, and what we want today is the spirit of unity amongst God's children, so that the Lord may work."[15]

If Moody did see the mission churches as driving a wedge between social classes, it seems plausible that he was concerned with the authenticity of the church's love rather than pretending to be kind while building a wealth-based hierarchy. Moody was not advocating for faith without works or suggesting that wealthy Christians should not provide for the poor. He merely desired to see wealth used to convey God's love to the world and not as a purely humanitarian, promotional, or even profit-making effort. Moody knew true Christian love does not involve dropping money in the offering plate to showcase one's generosity. It involves embracing the poor, befriending them, and treating them as brothers and sisters in the faith without partiality.

Moody's convictions about the proclamation of God's word and the importance of impartiality and unity within the church came into conflict as he sought to hold integrated meetings in the South. Because of his deep disagreement with segregation in the South and the division it was sure to create within the church, Moody spoke out against prejudice.

---
14 *Public Opinion* vol 21 (1896), 801.
15 Moody, *Secret Power*, 109.

An 1890 article discusses Moody's comments at a student conference in Northfield. Moody "warned his hearers that the common use of the term 'heathen,' in speaking of the Chinese, Japanese and Orientals, must be avoided in the exercises of the conference."[16] The report went on to note Moody's "suggestion that America has quite as much to answer for as China and India," referencing that "it is only in this generation that we have succeeded in abolishing slavery, more unchristian and, in some of its phases, more inhuman than any institution known in 'heathen' lands."[17]

While Moody accommodated segregationists for a time, his patience ran out in 1895 during a series of meetings in Texas where "Moody openly defied Jim Crow and racial discrimination. He became outraged when he saw physical barriers separating blacks from whites…Moody thrust his 270-pound frame against the wooden railings."[18] From that point on, "Blacks and whites would no longer have separate seating arrangements at Moody's revival."[19] Moody understood the sins of the United States should not be forgotten or submerged under an exaggerated sense of national pride and called Christians to practice impartiality, to honor one another, and to pursue peace and unity in the body of Christ. While Moody's willingness to hold segregated campaigns may have helped "to sever the cords between social justice and evangelical revivalism," we must take care that we do not dismiss the basic convictions that drove D. L. Moody: the word of God and the power of the Holy Spirit were crucial for revival.[20]

Moody's statements during his interactions with pastors in Atlanta, as well as those about the use of the word "heathen" at the Northfield

---

16 New York Times. 5 July 1890.
17 New York Times. 5 July 1890.
18 Edward J. Blum, *Reforging the White Republic: Race, Religion, and American Nationalism 1865-1898* (Baton Rouge: Louisiana State University Press, 2005), 143-144.
19 Blum, *Reforging the White Republic*, 144.
20 Blum, *Reforging the White Republic*, 144.

conference, make clear his disapproval of racism and prejudice. They also demonstrate that Moody spoke out against prejudice even if he continued to allow prejudice during his segregated meetings. In addition, segregation within the church surely raised concerns similar to those he expressed regarding the Mission Churches. Southerners who supported segregation were not showing authentic Christian love by diminishing those made in God's image. At the same time, Moody believed that God's word and the conviction of the Holy Spirit were necessary to transform the hearts of sinners even when those sinners were part of the body of Christ. That conviction drove him to preach the Scriptures.

He did not believe preaching abstinence would result in fewer alcoholics, nor did he believe leaving those with deep prejudices to their own devices would result in a more impartial world. Even if it did, without Christ, those who stopped drinking or laid aside their prejudices would not be transformed. Individuals who surrendered themselves to the word of God and experienced the power of the Holy Spirit would have their hearts changed, and their behavior would follow. Preaching the word of God, encouraging the church to pray, exhorting believers to live in the power of the Spirit, and calling the church to remain unified and to love through practical acts of kindness were the common themes of Moody's ministry. Moody saw preaching God's word and encouraging the church toward reform as his role in healing the ongoing social ills that plagued the country.

In the case of his campaigns in the South, Moody accommodated the foolishness and partiality of those whites, including white Christians, who insisted on segregated meetings. He followed his conviction about the word's transforming power rather than taking a stand against what he viewed as rebelliousness.[21] Preaching the word was paramount because it was what Moody knew would challenge people to recognize their sin, to

---

21 New York Times. 11 Dec 1876.

repent, and to live in the light of God's truth. Surely, we must acknowledge that allowing segregated meetings likely fueled white animosity toward blacks. At the same time, we must recognize that preaching to sinners is simply part of what it means to proclaim God's word in a broken world.

UNDISTRACTED FROM WORK

Moody was a complex character living in a uniquely complex time in the history of the United States. His theological convictions drove his decisions. Yet, like all of us, he was subject to the circumstances in which he did his work. He was incomplete and sought to be what God required him to be throughout his lifetime. He was faithful and flawed.

Moody was undistracted from the work God had called him to do, yet being undistracted does not guarantee perfection. His unrelenting focus on the power of God's word and the work of the Holy Spirit to transform human hearts led Moody to make choices in opposition to his contemporaries. Looking back at the history of racism in the United States, we may well wish that Dwight Moody had made different decisions. Perhaps if someone with Moody's influence had taken a stand against segregation, the church would have begun to address the divisions that continue to hinder us from showcasing the "manifold wisdom of God" today (Eph. 3:10 ESV). However, we must recognize that we, like Dwight Moody, continue to long for the transformation that comes by hearing God's word and yielding to the Holy Spirit.

Despite his inability to be all things to all people at all times, it is difficult to deny the importance of Moody's focus on the gospel throughout his life and ministry. He believed that any action taken in the world should lean back upon the power of God. He was not advocating for the church to set aside political matters but for the people of God to recognize that the social and political battles of the day were spiritual at their root and required Christians to fight with spiritual weapons.

He was not affirming prejudices and partiality—he longed to unify the church under the authority of God's word. Even with the divisive decisions he made, it would be unwise of us to dismiss Moody's desire to depend upon the Lord and his strength. As the psalmist says,

> You are my King and my God, who decrees victories for Jacob. Through you we push back our enemies; through your name we trample our foes. I put no trust in my bow, my sword does not bring me victory; but you give us victory over our enemies, you put our adversaries to shame. In God we make our boast all day long, and we will praise your name forever (Ps. 44:4–8 NIV).

HOW WE CAN BECOME UNDISTRACTED

Ultimately, being undistracted doesn't mean that we will make decisions that are always well-received. At times, we can focus so narrowly on good things that we act in ways that do not reflect God to the world. Still, being undistracted is crucial to the Christian life. As Paul notes,

> Therefore we do not lose heart. Though outwardly we are wasting away, yet inwardly we are being renewed day by day. For our light and momentary troubles are achieving for us an eternal glory that far outweighs them all. So we fix our eyes not on what is seen, but on what is unseen, since what is seen is temporary, but what is unseen is eternal (2 Cor. 4:16–18 NIV).

We focus, or fix, our attention on God and the things of God. We do not chase solutions that seek to better the world yet deny the spiritual battles we fight. To do so is to deny God his rightful place as Sovereign. Instead, as God's people, we long to be undistracted as we look at the world with eyes of faith.

LEARNING TO BE UNDISTRACTED

STEP 1: EMBRACE PSALM 1.

We need to cultivate a love for God's instruction by meditating on it day and night. When we have within us a deep, abiding sense that God has conveyed unparalleled wisdom through his word, we will be less likely to substitute God's wisdom with wisdom from other sources. Love for God's word is a necessary precursor to becoming undistracted.

STEP 2: RETHINK TIME.

The urgencies of the day are seldom as urgent as we seem to think. Christians won't fix the world. In fact, we "will leave the world broken, perhaps more broken despite our faithful efforts to live out the kingdom of God within it."[22] Our relatively short lives may feel limiting to us, but they do not limit the work God can do. He is not subject to time but works across the various generations of his people. Once we recognize that (a) the world is not ours to fix and (b) our primary task is to love God by obeying his commands (1 John 5:3), we can adopt a new posture in the world. That new posture does not react to the urgencies of the day but to the urgency of obedience.

It is certainly right to feel a sense of urgency to share the gospel or to engage in activities that seek to reform the social and individual wrongs that diminish those made in the image of God, yet "we are wrong… to think that the patient acts of prayer and fasting, the emotive cry of lamentation, or the slow, thoughtful engagement of the Scriptures and development of rich theology are not appropriate expressions of such urgency."[23] In other words, to be undistracted, we must commit

---

[22] Spencer, *Thinking Christian*, 38.
[23] Spencer, *Thinking Christian*, 38.

ourselves to an unyielding pursuit of God and an unwavering confidence that it is God's work in and through us rather than our own efforts that will transform the world. It is God who will make all things new (Rev 21:5). Our role is to live rightly before God. As Peter writes, "Since all these things are to be destroyed in this way, what sort of people ought you to be in holy conduct and godliness, looking for and hastening the coming of the day of God…" (2 Pet. 3:11–12 NASB).

STEP 3: ACCEPT OUR OWN LIMITATIONS.

The Christian life does not demand perfection. Instead, it assumes confession (1 John 1:9). We will not only miss the mark, but we will pursue misdirected desires as we seek to represent God to the world. While the Christian faith entails certain unwavering convictions, knowing Jesus does not mean we suddenly know everything. Our failures and shortcomings do not suggest that we are beyond hope but that, having been redeemed, we can depend on God and others to navigate a fallen world full of people who are faithful and flawed.

WALK IN THE WORD

"Therefore, since we are surrounded by such a great cloud of witnesses, let us throw off everything that hinders and the sin that so easily entangles. And let us run with perseverance the race marked out for us, fixing our eyes on Jesus, the pioneer and perfecter of faith. For the joy set before him he endured the cross, scorning its shame, and sat down at the right hand of the throne of God. Consider him who endured such opposition from sinners, so that you will not grow weary and lose heart."

– Hebrews 12:1-3 NIV

Hebrews 11 begins with a simple description of faith. It is "the assurance of things hoped for, the conviction of things not seen" (Heb. 11:1 ESV). By faith, "the people of old received their commendation" (Heb. 11:2 ESV). Abel, Enoch, Noah, Abraham, Sarah, Isaac, Jacob, Joseph, Moses, Rahab, and a host of others chose to take a risk and trust God instead of man. They chose to make their decisions based not upon what they saw before them but to trust in the God who is not limited by "things that are visible" (Heb. 11:3 ESV).

Outside of Abel (Gen. 4:1-8), Enoch (Gen. 5:24), and Rahab (Josh. 2:1–24), who make relatively short appearances in the Old Testament, each of the individuals listed in Hebrews 11 have moments when their actions seem to be driven less by faith and more by sight. Sarah and Abraham see no other way to obtain an heir than through Hagar (Gen. 16:1–16). Jacob wrestles with God for God's blessing prior to meeting Esau upon Jacob's return to Canaan (Gen. 32:22–32). Moses' initial attempt to address Israel's oppression by killing one of the Egyptians results in his fleeing to Midian (Exod. 2:11–16). Yet, in the end, these women and men demonstrate their commitment to live by faith.

Living by faith doesn't mean that we divorce ourselves from the concerns of the world. We don't turn a blind eye to all that's happening around us. However, it may mean we don't always respond to the world's problems in the ways that the world might like or in ways the world will understand. As we make choices based on "things not seen," our decisions may not make sense to those examining our choices in the moment or looking back over our lives. Our decisions will often seem strange.

Moody faced difficult decisions as he sought to navigate the tumultuous times in which he ministered. Despite the criticism of his contemporaries, Moody continued forward. We cannot enter into his head or heart, but evidence suggests that he was deeply opposed to racism and deeply committed to proclaiming the gospel and promoting the unity of God's people.

Decisions, especially the difficult ones, aren't always easy, and they often come with consequences. When we walk by faith, we must anticipate that the unseen won't be visible to everyone. Walking by faith won't shield us from error or criticism. To persevere, we may have to set aside our own preferences and understandings of the way the world works along with our self-interest and agendas. But, to walk by faith is to embrace the insight Joseph shared with his brothers: what man intends for evil, God can use for good (Gen. 50:20).

REFLECTION QUESTIONS

01 | While it is certainly right for us to hold one another accountable, we do need to take care not to demonize other members of Christ's body too quickly. How might we go about handling a situation in which someone we know seems to be making a poor choice?

02 | Are there instances in which you feel you've been overly critical of someone in the body of Christ because you didn't consider the role they were playing "by faith?"

03 | What does unity in the work of the Kingdom of God really look like? How might we think about the various tasks the body of Christ performs as being distinct yet unified?

04 | What do we need to do in order to prepare ourselves to walk by faith?

05 | Do all of us need to proclaim God's word in the same way?

06 | Having read about this characteristic of Dwight L. Moody, in what ways to you think you walk by faith? By sight?

07 | What do you envision changing about the way you live your life to walk by faith?

To move towards becoming "undistracted" in the ways of God, I will:

10
BECOMING USEFUL TO GOD

> "My earnest prayer is that God may make you not only his but a very useful man."
>
> – D. L. Moody,
> *personal correspondence with son William R. Moody*

God is not done with Dwight L. Moody, and he is not done with us either. Looking back over some of the characteristics that allowed God to use Moody reveals that the man was more than a humble evangelist. He had a deep concern that the people of God be useful to God. Moody specifically addresses the importance of developing usefulness in correspondence with his family. In an 1895 letter to his son, Paul, Moody writes, "If you go on for the next sixteen years improving as you have the last you will be a very useful man and that is the earnest prayer of your mother and father."[1] He encourages his daughter, Emma, to grow in usefulness, noting that being useful "is all there is to life anyway."[2] Clearly, being useful to God was of central concern to Mr. Moody.

USEFUL IN THE CHURCH

Being useful involves the work and the Word. Moody wanted to see Christians contributing to the ministry of the church. The work of ministry plays a crucial role in Christian life. Work and usefulness were connected because "to be a useful, happy Christian, just get to work and do not go to sleep."[3]

However, work was not the first step. Study was. As Moody put it, "if we first study the Word and then go to work, we shall be healthy, useful Christians."[4] The work and the Word permeated much of Moody's ministry, including the organization of Northfield Seminary for Girls, which was created "to help and encourage them, to fit them in the best way for a happy and useful life, to bring them into close contact with

---

[1] D. L. Moody to Paul Moody, 1895, MFP Collection, D. L. Moody Center Digital Archives, https://archives.moodycenter.org/digital/collection/p17348coll1/id/1466/rec/1
[2] D. L. Moody to Emma Fitt, 1893, Yale Collection, D. L. Moody Center Digital Archives, https://archives.moodycenter.org/digital/collection/p17348coll1/id/2069/rec/1
[3] Moody, *New Sermons, Addresses, and Prayers*, 577.
[4] Moody, *Pleasure and Profit in Bible Study*, 8

the very Fountain of Life, from which they may draw freely for all their needs."[5]

Being useful was also about being available to God. As Moody suggests, "Education is all right as far as it goes, but if that is all you have, you will be a dead failure. What you need for God's work is an anointing of the Spirit."[6] He goes on to comment that F. B. Meyer became "one of the most useful men in the pulpit to-day" because he received the anointing of the Spirit.[7] He makes a similar point about George Mueller, who "became one of the most useful men of this century" after "the Spirit of God powerfully converted him."[8]

In the church, we certainly want people to be useful. We want people to know God's word and to be empowered by the Holy Spirit. We also want people to pursue usefulness with earnestness and urgency. Whenever we are too comfortable, distracted, willful, stubborn, or unaware, we will likely miss opportunities to develop the sort of characteristics that made Moody available to God's use. We must begin to see becoming useful as something we urgently need. We need to commit to being surrendered, prayerful, studious, humble, free from the love of money, passionate for the lost, empowered by the Spirit, and undistracted from the Christian mission.

USEFUL IN OUR HEARTS

As mentioned, many people accused Moody of promoting individual piety and neglecting broader social concerns. Moody certainly believed that transformation occurred in the hearts of individuals. He felt that the members of Christ's body needed to work together. They needed

---

5 *Handbook of the Northfield Seminary and the Mt. Hermon School*, (Chicago: Fleming H. Revell, 1889), 20.
6 Moody, *Short Talks*, 123.
7 Moody, *Short Talks*, 123.
8 Moody, *Short Talks*, 117.

to showcase God's wisdom by obeying his word and teaching others to do the same. Whatever other activities in the political or social realms may be appropriate for Christians, evangelism and discipleship are the primary means by which Christians participate in God's work of making all things new. It is through discipleship that Christians avoid the pitfalls of pursuing human agendas or tying God to them. We must take care not to confuse God's agendas for our own, even when we are addressing legitimate concerns.

Our individual usefulness is critical because, without it, we will continue to live within the limits of our own understanding, resources, and power. There is much good that humans can bring about in this world. It is surely possible for the world to become more just through human action. However, when justice is detached from God, we miss our ultimate purpose. If we commit ourselves to transforming the world without God, we separate the two greatest commandments. Love of neighbor cannot stand apart from love of God. To be useful is to allow our love for God to propel us to love our neighbor.

As we look at D. L. Moody and the characteristics that made him useful to God, we do not see a man who followed his own path. We see a man who was overshadowed by God for the sake of the gospel. He was a man who committed to becoming less so that God would become more (John 3:30). It is this example that we must follow if our deepest desire is to be useful to God. We must allow him to direct our paths, to empower us, and to shine through us so that the world gives him the glory. We must be convinced, as Moody was, that "what this world wants is true men and women, not great men, but true and honest and upright persons that God can use."[9]

---

[9] D. L. Moody to Henry Cutler, 1892, MFP Collection, D. L. Moody Center Digital Archives, https://archives.moodycenter.org/digital/collection/p17348coll1/id/606/rec/4